# A PERFECT
# **TRAGEDY**

# A PERFECT
# TRAGEDY

## *Finding Purpose in Pain, Loss, and Addiction*

### JASON LENNOX

Paperback ISBN: 979-8-9869658-0-2

Design by Weller Smith Design, LLC.

10 9 8 7 6 5 4 3 2 1

First Edition

Published by Jason Lennox.

www.JasonLennox.com

Printed in the United States of America

**To my Grammie Diane:**
When I got the heartbreaking news
just one week into treatment,
I knew I was facing a tragedy—
one that would propel me six feet from the ground
into life or death.
Thank heavens it was six feet above.
You must have known there was more to my story
because ever since that fateful Christmas Day
you've been my guiding light,
my perseverance,
my drive to do and be better, and
my reason to make damn sure I don't lose another;
not without a peaceful parting, anyway.
For all the times you brought me love and joy,
this one's for you, Grammie.

# CONTENTS

"

**OUR GREATEST GLORY IS NOT IN NEVER FALLING BUT IN RISING EVERY TIME WE FALL.**

CONFUCIUS

# INTRODUCTION

My name is Jason Lennox, and I'm one of the fortunate people who has found a path to and through recovery from drug and alcohol addiction. That path was rocky, blurry, and more challenging than any other I've ever traveled. I spent the first twelve years of my life struggling to find my way, always seeking something to soothe my pain. The next twelve years were given over to experimenting with drugs and alcohol and progressing through the worst stages of addiction. And for the past twelve years, I've been hard at work finding recovery and seeking purpose in all my being and doing. Before I lost everything I had to addiction, I had already seen its power at work as it slowly took the life of my father, who died of cirrhosis of the liver at the young age of thirty-nine. He was one of the unfortunate ones. My own journey brought me close to death on several occasions, and in truth, I welcomed and wished for it on some of my worst days.

Today, I believe in the power of authenticity to transform even the worst of situations into the greatest of victories. I also believe that service to others has the power to shift our perspectives, and it can be a vehicle for sustaining recovery and wellness. That's why I do what I do today—writing, speaking, and working in the behavioral healthcare industry to try to make a difference in the lives of those who are still struggling through the journey of addiction and recovery.

**Thankfully, I was given one last chance at treatment, which saved my life and saved a lot of pain for a lot of people.**

One of the greatest challenges our world faces around the topic of addiction is breaking through misconceptions, misunderstandings, and ignorance. There are days it seems that challenge is greater than the struggle of overcoming the disease itself. Much of our society is very literal and logical when thinking and communicating about addiction, but addiction is not logical. Those who have never struggled with addiction often believe that if someone doesn't want the trouble that comes with drugs and alcohol, they should simply avoid taking a drink or drug. That's what I always heard. But for someone struggling to get or stay sober, that belief is one of the deadliest. Like the old War on Drugs catchphrase, "Just say no," people consistently oversimplify the reality of getting sober. And that line of thinking is so dangerous for those who are struggling, often destroying any chance they may have to get sober. In my worst of times, while I was trying everything I could to break free from addiction and failing miserably, hearing how "simple" it really should have been to get sober made me think there was something seriously wrong with my morality.

My progression, one that is common among others strug-gling with addiction, went something like this: I used drugs and alcohol and got into trouble. People told me to stop, and I tried, but it wasn't that simple. I used more drugs and alcohol and got into more trouble. People told me to stop, I wanted to stop, and I tried harder, but I couldn't. To cope with my failed attempts, I used more drugs and alcohol and got into more trouble. I was disowned, I was looked down on, I felt like a laughingstock. I knew so many people saw me as a kid who "chose" to live a lifestyle of pain and trouble. The only way I knew to cope with the embarrassment, shame, and guilt was to use more drugs and alcohol, and of course I got into even more trouble. As the pattern repeated itself, over time I succumbed to the belief that there was no way out for me. Thankfully, I was given one last chance at treatment, which saved my life and saved a lot of pain for a lot of people.

But not everyone gets there—in fact, most don't. A leading reason for that is that people are terrified to talk about having a problem. Most people find it incredibly challenging to share their realities. I did. It was only after being backed into one final corner of hell that I was able to share enough with one person to open the doors to treatment. Our world needs more of that kind of person—willing to listen without judgment, and able to believe that people can and do change.

If we are to change the way we tackle this problem, our society needs to hear about addiction and recovery a lot more than it does. If we do not turn a corner, we're going to lose millions of lives over the next several years. Millions. Drugs and alcohol are killing nearly a quarter million people per year in the United

States alone. The world needs significant help to change that. It needs more people who are willing to share their stories, and more people who are willing to listen. It needs you. It needs me. It needs all of us. This is why I've chosen to share my story so widely and loudly. It's important for people to understand that addiction isn't some sort of moral failure, and recovery is possible. I hope, as you read through this memoir, you'll consider how you might find your own chance at recovery, or help others in your life find recovery, and make a difference in the world for those who need your compassion most.

"

# ADDICTION IS THE ONLY PRISON WHERE THE LOCKS ARE ON THE INSIDE.

UNKNOWN

# THE END OF
# THE ROAD

I woke up to the bright light above my bed, which elimi-
nated any hope that this was just a nightmare. That was a
familiar feeling. I grasped the thin, plastic-covered pillow and
turned over to block out the light. The mattress was just as
thin, two inches at most. The anxiety was unbearable. I sat up
instead. The walls were brick, gray, and cold. They were a representation of my life, and just as claustrophobic as my current
circumstances.

I wore an orange jumpsuit, a pair of boxers, and an undershirt that smelled like they had been in a wet basement for
months. My toilet was in plain sight of anyone walking by, just
inches from my sink. The metal fixtures matched the walls,
cold and gray. The open floor space was about five feet by seven
feet; enough room to turn around and not much more. Sitting

7

on the bed, I had so many questions. How had this happened? How did I end up with this life? There I sat, twenty-four years old, locked up again, and this time it was different. There was no release date. There was no talking my way out of this one. This was the end of the road. Realization set in. I, a kid who'd had so much potential and so many opportunities in life, now had no hope for a reasonable future. In fact, I didn't want a future anymore. I wanted my life to end. I couldn't live with the pain, the suffering, and the guilt. I didn't have it in me to face the reality of my situation. I had been on the run for nearly a year, with felony warrants out for my arrest. I was in some serious trouble.

The hardest pill to swallow was the feeling that now everyone knew who I really was. I thought I had hidden it well. I was wrong. And thanks to the sobriety brought on by my stays in the hospital and detention center, I had lost the comforting oblivion that had saved me for so long. Even I knew who was sitting in that cell—a serious danger to himself and others, a waste of what could have been a valuable life, a shell of a human being. I knew there was no chance to restore what could have been. I looked around the cold cell again. What could I use to end the pain? I needed a way out. I thought of all the points along the way where something could have shifted, all the decisions that could have been made differently. The knowledge that everything I was experiencing could have been avoided only made me feel worse. All I'd had to do was clean my life up. Why couldn't I, someone so smart in other ways, have kicked a habit that brought nothing but pain and suffering? But back in my current reality, it didn't really matter. The air coming from the vents gave me goose bumps. I grabbed the sheetlike blanket and dropped back down on the mattress. I prayed to God that the next time I opened my eyes, I would have a different life. But it wouldn't come. Not that day.

My mind drifted back to the hospital, where I had woken up the day before, and to the long road that had led me there. I remembered the moments after I had called emergency services, as I began fading from consciousness. I had made it to the driveway, and I was looking deep into the night sky—a dark sky that seemed like it was closing in. The vastness grew smaller and smaller with each blink of my eyes. The brightness of the stars was dimming. The wonder of what was out there, what was still to be discovered, and of the life that could have been—all fading away into the darkness of the night. There I lay, defeated once and for all by addiction, under the sky of a universe that had once presented so much promise and wonder. While emergency personnel took my body to the emergency room for saving, the universe carried my soul back to the night sky where it had all started. Back to the beginning.

> **The hardest pill to swallow was the feeling that now everyone knew who I really was.**

# "

# DO NOT FEEL LONELY, THE ENTIRE UNIVERSE IS INSIDE OF YOU.

RUMI

# CHAPTER 2

# THE BEGINNING

It was a warm summer night, and the air smelled like freshly cut grass. I was young, somewhere between infant and toddler, lying in a car seat in the back of a pickup truck, staring into the crisp and clean black sky. It was so dark, yet so bright, and filled with stars radiating life. The brightness was overwhelming, yet easy to look at, a hope of sorts. The wonder hit me. What's out there? How far does it travel? What's possible in all that darkness, in all that light? It was dark, I was alone and barely old enough to make a peep, yet there was no fear. Just a deep sense of awe and appreciation, and a vision of a world too large and endless to comprehend. No fear, just freedom and a sense of endless possibility.

I've found myself recalling this vivid childhood incident throughout my life, yet I could never determine whether it was reality or a dream. Either way, it is a long-lasting memory that seems to contradict human nature: A baby boy, all alone in the dark night, yet full of peace, comfort, and imagination. As I've recalled this memory throughout the years, I have always returned to one question: What happened? How did that little child, so full of hope in all the darkness, turn into such a terrified, hopeless soul, filled with so much fear and despair?

"

# I THINK YOU NEVER FORGET YOUR CHILDHOOD, WHETHER IT WAS HAPPY OR UNHAPPY.

MARCEL CARNE

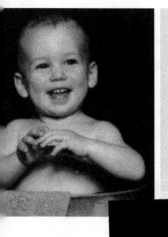

# CHAPTER 3

# THE CLIMB

My life began in 1986 in Springfield, Massachusetts. I had an older brother, born the year prior. Mom and Dad were both young—in their late teens and early twenties, respectively. Mom was beautiful, with brown-blond hair down to her shoulders, bright blue eyes, and a sharply defined jaw. Dad was a handsome man, with dark brown curls, high cheekbones, and a smile that brought dimples to his face. They looked like a perfect couple together. They were still trying to figure out their lives, and drugs and alcohol didn't help those efforts. In fact, my dad was probably already plagued with the disease of addiction by this time. He'd had a tough childhood, losing his mother to cancer when he was thirteen and dealing with his own father's struggles with alcoholism. Mom and Dad didn't always get along. We bounced around a bunch as young children, finally landing in Minnesota in 1988. About a year later, my dad moved back to Massachusetts, leaving Mom, my brother, and me behind in Minnesota with a bit of a hole in our lives.

My mom found a new partner to fill the father-figure role, to an extent. My stepdad, Dale Sr., was an old-school guy who expected respect, hard work, and obedience to any rules he set forth. He had curly, red-brown hair that stuck out in a bit of an Afro and dropped down his neck. He was short, skinny but muscular, and had faded tattoos covering half his arms. He rode a Harley-Davidson motorcycle that was about twice his size. He and my mom went on to have two kids, giving me a younger brother and a sister. After about eight years together, my mom and stepdad married; on the outside, they seemed to be a perfect match. But on the inside, things weren't always so perfect.

Control was a huge part of our household dynamic. My mom and stepdad argued often, each looking for the last word and a bit more power over the other. That mentality trickled down to the kids, too. Everything had to be done to perfection, and if it wasn't, my brother and I would get a grounding and a good whooping. I remember I would wait for my parents to arrive after a day of doing chores, hoping we had done a good enough job. My body would tighten up as they walked through the door as I wondered what they might be thinking. Sometimes the inadequacy of our work meant we'd have to redo everything; other days it meant we'd get whooped, and some days, what we'd done was deemed okay. All the while, I was learning that I must always be looking to perfect things and avoid negative consequences.

That mindset took hold early on in school, too. I enjoyed going to school, but soon everything changed. I remember showing up to preschool one day in my favorite outfit of green corduroy overalls. I then had an accident, and the overalls were soaked in urine. It crushed me. How could I do something like that, especially in a public setting? I thought everyone now knew that something was wrong with Jason Lennox. It was the beginning of an uphill climb to show others I was not an embarrassment. As a young boy, I was ready for that climb. Or so I thought.

> I felt like I was always wrong at home, but school was within my control.

I remember sitting in my third-grade math class preparing for one of our weekly tests. Mr. Reichart was explaining the rules, but I hardly heard him. My hands got sweaty, my heart started racing, and my brain went into overload. It was like waiting for the starting gun in a track meet. I was in the zone. I knew I had to finish that test first, and I knew I had to finish it without a single question wrong. My self-worth depended on it. I felt like I was always wrong at home, but school was within my control. "And, begin," Mr. Reichart instructed. The test was timed, with a mix of addition, subtraction, multiplication, and division problems laid out in rows and columns. I flew through row one and picked up the pace. My nervous system was exploding, like it did watching the final two minutes of my favorite sports team trying to make a comeback. When I was done, I raised my hand and looked around. All the other kids were still working. What a relief. One stage down, one to go. Mr. Reichart took my test and began correcting. I watched anxiously, hoping to get it back without *any* red on it. Red marks signified something bad—they meant I wasn't good enough, again. They meant something was wrong with me.

I watched Mr. Reichart finishing with my test, his gray hair and glasses bent over the paper. The anticipation was unbearable. My body was tight, my brain was loose, and I felt a sense of impending doom all around. He started walking my way and quietly dropped the powerful piece of paper on my desk. The moment I saw the words "Great job!" and "30/30," I felt an overwhelming sense of relief. Not accomplishment—relief. The grade signified that there was nothing wrong with me, and I felt I could exist again. My shoulders lowered, my face loosened, and I sank into my desk chair, watching the rest of the class finish their tests with a few moments of what felt like sincere satisfaction.

This early cycle of anxiety and relief would come to plague my life. I didn't know any other way to be in the world. Up and down, up and down, up and down. I would expend more energy in some hours than most people probably do in a day. It was all to serve a purpose—to satisfy my deep-seated feelings of inferiority, inadequacy, and unworthiness.

As a young child, I committed to doing and being big things when I grew up. I wanted to be a professional athlete, then a sports analyst, and eventually a business owner. I even thought it might be cool to be president. No matter where I ended up, I knew I had to amount to something, and I made commitments to stay away from drugs and alcohol, to never smoke a cigarette, to excel in school, and to avoid trouble at home. With my deep need to show the world I was worthy of it, I bounced between trying my hardest and wanting to give up. As I got older, that fight got harder and harder; I learned I couldn't be perfect at everything, and I believed that said something about me. As an elementary school–age kid, I had already started to question whether living was for me or not.

I was ten years old when my internal debate came to a head for the first time. We had just moved into an enormous new house. A gravel driveway separated our blue wood-sided home from the neighbor's, and there was a basketball court in front of the garage. Inside, there was enough space to run for days. Our family of six, plus as many pets, had just come from a three-bedroom home with about half the square footage. This was a dream home, comparatively speaking. But even in the dreamiest of homes, life can look different on the outside than it is on the inside. As I sat in the kitchen, my mind swirled with thoughts about how hard it seemed for me just to be normal—to interact with people, get life right, and stay out of trouble at home. Even waking up many days was harder than I thought it should be. I stood next to the stove, with light beaming in through the kitchen's many windows. I looked up and saw a knife block on the counter, and suddenly I had a peculiar thought. I grabbed one of the biggest knives, lifted it up, and turned it toward my chest. I pushed it against the center of my breastbone, resting just an inch or two away from my major organs. My heart raced, my eyes widened, and I felt the poke of the tip come through my shirt. The room was empty of all sound and energy. I felt a certain peace and calm I wasn't used to. Maybe, I thought, that was what the end of life felt like. It was freeing, a few moments of reprieve from my daily fight to do enough. I had only one thought for the next minute or so: *I wonder how much it would hurt before it was over?* Fear of the pain crippled me. My legs shook a little, and as quickly as I could, I threw the knife onto the counter. It was as if the room was spinning around me. What had just happened? I thought there must have been something terribly wrong with me. I ran outside and grabbed a basketball to escape the moment.

As it turned out, I was pretty good at basketball. Our family didn't have the resources for me to play a lot of organized sports, but I had a neighbor who was a few years older who taught me how to shoot, dribble, and play the game. We had a lot of fun together, and he called me "All-Star." That made me feel a little better about myself. The fact that someone believed in me was striking. I began to realize that sports provided the potential for me to show others I held value in this world.

My elementary school would hold track meets, which became a source of great joy in my life. Those who finished first or second in any event went on to the all-city track meet—the big stage. The year I turned ten, I cruised through the school track meet and placed in the top two in all events. There were about four weeks until the all-city meet, and I counted down every single day. As the city event neared, I could barely sleep due to excitement. I knew the citywide meet was going to put me on a larger stage; it was a chance to show a lot of new people I was worthy.

The morning of the city meet, I had just one thing on my mind: winning. I counted down the hours and minutes with my thoughts racing, my heart beating harder and faster. I knew I needed to get through the school day, but it was incredibly hard to focus or even have a normal conversation. By the time evening arrived, it felt like it had been the longest day ever, and my excitement was overwhelming. As I watched some of the other events get started, I envisioned myself taking to the track. I was participating in four events: the triple jump, the fifty-meter hurdles, the hundred-meter sprint, and the mile run. The running races were the ones I was anticipating most, because all the participants started on one line, in front of one crowd, waiting for one gunshot. They were a chance to stand in the spotlight and show the world who I was.

Finally, the moment for the hurdle race arrived. Like a tiger waiting to be let out of a cage, I leaned forward, and it took a strong effort to stop myself from jumping the gun. The world felt silent and calm. Maybe that moment of quiet peace, such a far cry from the anxiety of my usual life, was what drew me to the sport. With my heart racing, my mind laser-focused, and my imagination envisioning a first-place finish, I paused in a moment of stillness. Then, with a loud boom and a dash of energy all around, the gun went off. I ran, jumped, ran, jumped, and then, as quickly as it had all started, it was over—I clipped one of the hurdles with my shoe and crashed to the ground. I ran to the grass in the middle, tears streaming down my face. My older brother met me and consoled me. He asked where it hurt and I pointed to the scrapes on my knee, but that was a lie. Where it hurt most was in my head. After all that buildup, all the waiting and anticipating, instead of showing the world how good I was, I had confirmed what my inner voice had known all along—that I was worthless and would never be good enough.

In school, I continued to try to prove my value by campaigning for president of the student council. When I won, I was invited to eat lunch with the principal, and I remember feeling a whole new level of importance. *Maybe*, I thought, *I am worth something after all.* But back at home, things felt different. My mom and stepdad fought regularly, and most nights I sat in my room wondering if life would always make me feel so anxious. I was living in two worlds—one at school, where I could excel and prove myself, and another at home, where no matter what I did, I felt less-than. I was constantly afraid of experiencing the pain and suffering I knew were just around the corner. Feeding my ego, hurting my ego, feeding my self-worth, destroying my self-worth—the cycles continued and exhausted me. And with middle school just around the corner, where I'd be joining a new group of kids from many other schools, I knew I would have to start the process of proving my worth all over again.

...

My worst nightmares came true in middle school. I was the kid that was easy to pick on, and I felt I had brought it on myself. At the start of the year, we colored large name tags to place on our desks. On mine, I wrote my nickname—Star. That was my basketball mentor's name for me, short for "All-Star." But the name quickly transitioned from a compliment to a joke. The kids saw "Star" and started laughing and making jokes about it. I was crushed. I ripped the name tag down and started over, drawing a simple and plain version of my first name. It was then I realized authenticity and vulnerability were way too risky, even at school. I had always used school as an escape from all the worries and fears of home, but now school was no longer an escape. With a home that felt scary and crippling, this one crushing experience at school changed my whole world. Suddenly, I had no safe space.

I remember watching all the "cool" kids hanging out with girls, wearing fashionable JNCO pants, playing sports, and sitting together at lunch. I did everything I could to stay away. Not because I was a loner, but because it was easier to avoid being picked on that way. I assumed the other kids had it better than me, so I walked through life full of fear, worrying about what everyone else thought and waiting for the next Star incident. I kept my mouth closed and quickly learned to mind my business.

At home, my mom and stepdad had decided it was best to split up. Even though it had been chaotic and worrisome living together, it was still sad to see them separate. I saw the pain in my stepdad's eyes, and I knew our world was changing forever.

My mom bought a new house in a town about twenty-five miles away. I'll never forget the day we drove out to see it. I was filled with worry and sadness about moving as Mom navigated the winding country road. With my head smashed against the window, all I could see were miles and miles of fields. The sun was setting, the fields were empty, and a depression set in like never before. There was nothing around. No hope. No future. It was suffocating. I didn't want a life like this. But suddenly, as if I had an angel on my shoulder tapping my brain, a thought came to me. *What if I could be somebody in this new school?*

# "

# NO MATTER HOW HARD THE PAST IS, YOU CAN ALWAYS BEGIN AGAIN.

BUDDHA

# CHAPTER 4

# A FRESH START

New Richland was a small town of around a thousand people. There were three other small towns, plus a bunch of townships, that all came together in one school district—New Richland–Hartland–Ellendale–Geneva. As I settled in and made friends with a couple of neighbors, I was excited about my new shot at life. But when school started at NRHEG, that excitement faded quickly. In my first days, I realized that not only was this not going to be the fresh start I had hoped for, it was going to be *worse* than my last school. Every attempt I made to fit in seemed to have the opposite effect. My nickname went from Star to Slick thanks to the amount of hair gel I used to try to make myself look good. I resented the kids who made fun of me because they seemed to fit in so easily. And even more so, I resented myself for failing so badly.

Back home, I found some solace in one neighbor friend who still wanted to hang out. Thankfully, he went to the high school and I was at the middle school, otherwise, I'm certain he'd have joined the fun at my expense. His name was Dustin, and he was short, skinny, and had sandy blond hair. He lived about seven houses down on the same side of the road as me. He introduced me to another friend of his, Chris, who lived just outside the town line. He was tall and skinny, had a long oval face, and greasy straight-hair that fell in front of his eyes. Chris and I were in the same grade but hadn't interacted yet. We met in the middle of town, behind a white brick building. It was fall, and just starting to get a little colder. The grass was damp, the air was crisp, and we could see our breath slightly.

The three of us stood in a circle and the other two sparked up cigarettes. They offered me one. I had always promised myself, and everyone else around me, I'd never do drugs, drink, or smoke. But in the moment, none of that mattered. I had an opportunity to expand my network of new friends from one to two. I grabbed the cigarette from Chris's hand and fired it up. It tasted awful. A strong menthol cigarette was no easy way to start a habit. After a handful of puffs, Chris looked at me and asked, "Why don't you inhale?" I replied with, "I am, see?" He kindly showed me that inhaling meant breathing in through my mouth, not my nose, after taking a puff. I followed suit, and the rush of smoke into my system, and what felt like my brain, about knocked me to the ground. It didn't take long before I felt nauseous. I had to sit down. The other two sure got a kick out of that sight, laughing as I crumpled in front of them. I felt the need to lie down, so I ended up walking home alone. I remember telling myself that smoking was something I'd never do again. The feeling was horrible and certainly not worth it. But as it turned out, when the discomfort was weighed against feeling accepted and like I belonged, the cigarettes were going to win.

In the beginning, sickness almost always followed my experiences with chemicals, but it didn't matter—they were my way of finally fitting in somewhere in life. The kids who were offering me cigarettes, drugs, and alcohol didn't put me down—at least not most of the time—they didn't care what I said or looked like. And they were actually a lot of fun. But the truth is, addiction had already begun working its way into my life long before that first cigarette. The psychological factors that would lead me to seek relief in substance use had been slowly taking hold all through my childhood. So when I found this group of kids willing to accept me as one of their own, I held on as tightly as I could.

Eventually, the drugs and alcohol weren't as sickening, and I began to have a little more fun. As my first year in New Richland wound down, life had become a little more bearable, but with the new friends and habits came more trouble. My grades fell dramatically. I had been a straight-A student for most of my life, and suddenly I was failing every class except gym. My older brother was in similar trouble and struggling in school, so my mom decided to send us to Massachusetts for a couple weeks. Our primary purpose: to find our father and have a hard look at what life had to offer on the other side of trouble, drugs, and alcohol.

I hadn't seen or heard from my father at all since he returned to the East Coast when I was just a couple years old. I never knew the whole story, but I remember my mom telling us he was sick. I didn't have any sufficient memories or even pictures of him, so I had no idea what to expect when we flew out that spring to stay with our aunts Dana and Mayra. Dana, my father's oldest sister, was a well-kept woman, short and round with trim, gray-brown hair. Mayra, her partner, was also short and round but had shoulder-length brown hair. She was Puerto Rican, with a voice that was raspy and animated. They were the first women I'd ever been around who were married to each other. Dana and Mayra had taken care of us when we were younger and our parents were struggling, and now they welcomed us like we had never left. On our first night in their large, beautiful home, with its shiny hardwood floors, comfortable furniture, full kitchen, and knickknacks all over, I remember being anxious. Though the home was as welcoming as any, I didn't know how to respond to my aunts' warm personalities. They were very loving and expressive and wanted hugs and kisses all the time. Those were such foreign behaviors to me that I felt incredibly uncomfortable. Retreating to my sleeping space that night was a relief. The next morning, my aunt told us no one could get ahold of my dad. But they had a plan—as it turned out, quite a familiar one. They'd call around to the local detoxes and treatment centers until they found him. They told us he was sick and needed help, and that maybe he was at one of those places for treatment. Sure enough, they found him at a detox facility up the road. They asked if we'd be okay going to see him there. We had no idea what it would be like, but our purpose was to see him, so of course we wanted to go.

My brother and I were called into the visiting room, where we sat watching other families and patients interact. I had no recollection of what my father looked like, and I remember sitting in that chair wondering which of the men walking through the doors was him. The anticipation was overwhelming; all the commotion and other conversations in the room faded away as I watched the door. In my mind's eye, I imagined my father as short and skinny, with cropped brown hair and a bit of an ever-present half smile. I couldn't find anyone matching that description. Then suddenly, a woman in scrubs was heading our way, with her arm wrapped around a tall, skinny man. His long, dark brown hair fell in a ponytail down to the bottom of his shoulder blades, and he was balding on the top. My body grew very tense. I sat up in my chair, my legs locked and my hands grasping each other strongly. This man wasn't anything like I had pictured. But it was him. They sat down in a chair across from us, and what felt like minutes passed in silence. I was so uncomfortable and scared, and as I looked at him, all I could think was that he wasn't normal. He struggled to keep his eyes open. His hair was full of white, crusty chunks, and he wore a gown that was full of white stains, too. It looked like he had been drooling for days. The nurse broke the silence.

"John, these are your sons. Would you like to say hi?"

He looked up and it wasn't clear if he understood. He muttered, "Hi." I don't remember how long we sat there, but I do remember the awkwardness never went away, and we left that visit knowing something was terribly wrong. My aunt told us he'd come by as soon as he left the facility, and that he'd be in better shape then. She was always so gracious with him. She told us he was sick, but that he could get better, and that she thought he would, knowing his children were in town.

It turned out my aunt was right, because we spent some good time with my father over the next couple weeks. He was intelligent, funny, and generous in his ways. Most nights, though, he'd leave to go home, and we knew he was likely off to drink to relieve what was going on inside. His illness was apparent through his actions and physical appearance. I later found out that by this point, the doctors had diagnosed him with early-stage cirrhosis, a disease that essentially eats away at the liver over time. Cirrhosis usually results from heavy drinking, and that was the case with my father. I can't imagine what it must have been like to hear a deadly diagnosis at the age of thirty-six. But there was hope—the doctors told my father that if he could kick the drinking habit, the disease wouldn't progress and he could probably live a good, lengthy life. There isn't a much greater motivation than that—life over death. It's at our core to fight for survival. But my father had even more motivation than the doctor's orders on his side: My mom had invited him to come stay with us in Minnesota. She told him she would house him, feed him, and not expect anything in return, but there was just one stipulation—no drinking.

I was only in middle school at the time, and I ignorantly assumed it was a simple calculation: His kids plus his life would be more valuable than the bottle. And at first that's how it seemed to go. He moved out to Minnesota and began to repair what he could in his relationships with my brother and me. It was so refreshing to start putting the pieces of such a mysterious puzzle together. We got to know our dad and spent a lot of time hanging with him. Even my friends loved coming over to visit with him. He was just like one of us, causing trouble and letting his inner child out. One day, we were hitting golf balls through the backyard, aiming toward the highway. We'd challenge each other to hit the cars as they drove by, but it was such a long shot we rarely came close. After my dad joined in, though, one of the balls I hit pelted a car driving by. We watched the car drive down the highway and turn toward our street. We all ran for cover and left my dad to deal with the upset driver. Afterward, he was mad at all of us, but it was a different kind of mad than we were used to. We had grown up fearing the kind of mad that oftentimes meant a whoopin' with the belt or days-long groundings; it was a fear that ruled all other feelings. But it wasn't like that with my dad. After a short while, he laughed and we continued with our day. I knew I could get used to that kind of relationship. I felt a satisfaction I had been longing for. With Mom and Dad together again— although not intimately—there was a sense of relief and peace in my life. I began to forget about all the shortcomings, defects, and flaws I believed made me less than everyone else. Maybe that's where it all had come from all along—feelings of abandonment that hadn't even been realized. With my dad back, I didn't have everything I wanted, but I had a missing piece, one half of a large puzzle, back in my life. Then there was the day I'll never, ever forget.

I came home from school one afternoon and didn't immediately see my dad. My mom sat my brother and me down and told us he was gone, on a bus back to Massachusetts. Apparently, the life he had been building in Minnesota with his children, without alcohol, wasn't in the cards anymore. I looked at my brother, sitting across from me with a long face, tightlipped as usual. It was hard to read my brother. My thoughts swirled and I couldn't grasp what was happening inside. Just as quickly as the relationship had begun, it was over. I had only been getting to know my dad for a couple months. How could he walk away from his children, I wondered. How could he give us up—even give up the chance to prolong his life—all for drinking? My heart sank, my body shook, my eyes welled up with tears, and within minutes, I felt an overwhelming sense of dissatisfaction and unworthiness return. Like a tingling sensation, the feeling was physical and ran from head to toe. Again, life had proven I wasn't good enough. Not even for the man who helped create me. I went to my room and sat in silence, looking around. The small room had two beds, one in the middle and the other protruding from the half closet. I sat on the big bed and shed a few tears. But behind the tears, and more prevalent than my sadness, was an anxiety for this man I'd never really known. My time with him was a roller coaster of a couple months, and I wondered if I'd ever have a couple more. Staring out through the window into the eastern sky, I imagined him on the bus, somewhere under that same sky, making his way back. Was he thinking about us? Did he feel what I felt? Would he come back? The sky was all sorts of colors—blue, yellow, purple, and pink—and though it was magnificent looking, I was full of depression. I had to find a way out of that feeling, and I knew just how to do it. I set off for my friend's place down the road.

...

By the end of my middle school years, I'd adapted to the drugs and alcohol and wasn't sick after every use. Marijuana was popular with most of the friends I hung out with. It created a cloudlike state of mind, fading in and out of full consciousness. While losing control of my consciousness was a bit frightening for me, it did relieve the feelings of anxiety, depression, unworthiness, discomfort, and the omnipresent sense of doom I had suffered from for so long. And the experience of smoking pot was sometimes just as nice as the emotional relief. The ritual of it—holding the little pipe, watching the lighter flicker on and the pot turn bright red, taking in the smoke, coughing breaths of smoke out and passing it along to the next person—created a feeling of community I appreciated more each time we smoked. The laughing and fun that followed didn't hurt, either.

Then there was alcohol. One of the first times I ever got drunk was a warm summer night when I was about fourteen years old. It was already dark out, and my mom and her new boyfriend were in the bedroom for the evening. Until then, I had only drunk a couple times, and each instance it had just been a bit of hard liquor, which I found terrible. It was like poison; it burned going down, and it gave me heartburn that seemed to last for hours. My mom's boyfriend drank beer, though. On this night, feeling bored and searching for a better state of mind, I went to the fridge and grabbed a few bottles of Michelob Golden Draft Light. I retreated to the den at the front of our house, closed the door behind me, and sat down at the computer desk. I logged into the computer and started the dial-up connection to the internet. Back then, connecting to the internet could take minutes, so while I waited, I grabbed a bottle, twisted off the cap, and took my first swig. It didn't taste much better than the hard stuff, but it didn't burn like the hard stuff. The taste was sour. I took big gulps to power through. I stared into the computer screen, watching the connecting dots appear, disappear, appear, and disappear again. Another drink, another connection attempt. Finally, the internet was up, and the first bottle of beer was empty. I opened another and logged into MSN Messenger. In those early days of the internet, instant messaging with friends and classmates was the neatest thing. As I worked through the second bottle of beer, I felt an overwhelming sense of freedom. The night, my home, the environment—they all felt lighter. Even my arms felt lighter, as if I could lift them more easily. My brain made sense of everything around me. My body warmed, my arms and legs tingled a bit, and I could taste the summer night. The smell of freshly cut grass mixed with hot tar drifted through the front window. I sat in the chair, staring at the Messenger window, where a long list of kids I went to school with were active. I sparked conversations with several of them, something I'd never have done without the freeing influence of the beer. It felt liberating: I could finally be one of them. I belonged, at last. It was then that I knew—with this newfound help I'd discovered—I was going to fit in. It was going to be okay after all.

My early years of high school were a whirlwind of friends, sports, and fun. As a freshman football player, I suffered an incredibly scary injury, taking a helmet to the back that left me temporarily paralyzed. The doctors thought it might be best to avoid contact sports forever, but that didn't fit into my plans. Sports provided me with a huge stage and a channel through which I could show my worth. If that meant ignoring expert advice, so be it. I dove back into basketball as soon as I could, and when the varsity running back had a season-ending injury in my sophomore year, I returned to the football field. I was hanging out with the "cool" kids more, getting better at sports, and finding joy in all the fun that came with both. Life was happening, and it wasn't so miserable anymore.

Much to my surprise, as a successful running back, I soon caught the eye of one of the cheerleaders. Steph was medium height and skinny, with light brown, shoulder-length hair. She had freckles to complement a beautiful smile that caught the attention of anyone in sight. She laughed with so much joy and walked with her head held high. It was easy to see she meant business in life and that she had an amazing outlook. One Friday night, she and some friends stopped by my house. We had converted half my garage into a finished, insulated space where we could all hang out. The walls were unpainted plywood, but there was a sectional couch as well as a TV, DVD player, and game systems all powered by an extension cord coming from the house. We coined it "Da Crib," and it was the hot spot for our group of friends.

That night I went outside to pee, and Steph followed. She confronted me without fear, dropping a kiss on me I didn't expect or know how to handle. It lasted for what seemed like many minutes, and I felt a sense of connectedness, of love, and of being okay that I never knew was possible. The weight on my shoulders was gone. My heart was jumping. The dopamine rush to my brain enhanced every physical and emotional sensation. I had been seeking connection all through my younger years, but I could never have imagined that feeling. It was the most intimate feeling of acceptance I had ever experienced. It was as if everything I had ever hoped for came true in that ten-minute window. We went back inside, and I don't think I stopped smiling for the rest of the night. My friends knew. I knew. We all knew. Life had taken on a new meaning.

As I sat under the stars that night outside my garage, I breathed in the fresh air and realized life was giving me everything I had ever dreamed of. I was a rising-star football player with a cheerleader pursuing me and all the popular kids looking to me for fun and fellowship. It was the American Dream, like something out of the movies. My life had filled up quickly, and I felt that the world could finally see and recognize the good version of Jason Lennox. I rarely looked back, preferring to bury all the pain and misery from my past, but on that night, with stars lighting up the sky, I thought back to the kid I had been just a few years prior. The one who felt he couldn't amount to anything, the laughingstock of two different schools. I had been so depressed, anxious, and despairing that I had seriously doubted the purpose of living. And yet there I sat, experiencing what felt like the most satisfying life possible, with parties every weekend, hanging with friends, smoking pot, and drinking beer all week long. I felt secure, maybe for the first time

I could remember. My social status was as good as it could be, and I had found the key to relieving all the uncomfortable symptoms of being human. I felt the physical relief with every drink and hit I took. Life felt like a roller coaster, and I was on my way to the top, where I had always wanted to be. But I had forgotten that life, like every roller coaster, could only go so high before coming back down. The only question was how far I'd rise before the fall.

# "

# HE WHO WANTS EVERYTHING WILL LOSE EVERYTHING.

MEXICAN PROVERB

# CHAPTER 5

# ALL I EVER WANTED, GONE

**M**y junior year started with some trouble—I got busted for drinking and driving during football season and had to sit out the last half of the year. That crushed me, but even bigger trouble was brewing in my personal life. All I had ever wanted was a girlfriend, and now I had an incredibly loyal, beautiful, caring, and kind one by my side. But it wasn't enough—not if the sickness inside me, which was fueled partly by the early stages of addiction and partly by the hurt and pain I had never dealt with, ran my show. I had begun to take the good things in life for granted, with greed and ego leading my way. So when I saw an opportunity to date the most popular girl around, I jumped at it. My twisted thinking meant I was all about having and getting whatever was bigger, better, and faster.

When I broke things off with Steph, she was absolutely crushed. I was lying on my bed when she arrived to drop my belongings on the floor. "How could you do this?" she asked with a broken, quivering voice. While I could see the pain she was in, I didn't show remorse or offer any explanation. I just wanted to move on, and I was willing to do whatever I could, even at the expense of someone I cared about, to enhance my position and reach what I envisioned as a "better" stage of life. So I shut out Steph's crying with a trip to the garage, where I smoked some pot and drifted away to oblivion.

The relationship lasted about two weeks before my new catch left a breakup letter in my locker at school. I took the letter into the bathroom across the hall and trembled as I opened it. Each word was bolder, louder, and more damning than the next. My knees and legs shook and a sense of suffocation and despair took over. I quickly moved into a stall, sat down, and shut the door. I reread the letter, looking for any hope that the words could be turned around. The letter explained she thought I was a great guy but she just wasn't ready for a relationship. Each time I read it, a familiar feeling hit. I wasn't good enough. I wasn't good enough. I wasn't good enough. *Why wasn't I good enough?* I was paralyzed. My brain couldn't function, and my stomach knotted up. I couldn't leave that stall, which felt like it was getting smaller and smaller. I stared at the white walls and thought about Steph, maybe for the first time since the breakup. She would never have done this. She would have done anything she could have to make me happy, and I had let her go. For the first time in a long while, I felt the familiar sensations I had experienced so often as a child—overwhelming fear and anxiety, unworthiness, and defeat. It was just a fraction of what was to come.

As I fumbled through the coming days, school felt like a daily reminder of the end of all my dreams. My ex wouldn't even talk to me and had already moved on. I watched my friends, one by one, distance themselves from me. Guilt, shame, and regret had always been part of my life, but this felt different. I struggled with the knowledge that I had achieved everything I had ever dreamed of, and then had thrown it all away in the name of greed. My days and nights were full of remorse, self-pity, and depression. The world became a little bit darker, a little more hopeless. As I tried to numb the pain, drugs and alcohol became an increasingly regular part of my life. But they couldn't completely erase my sense of loss, and there was more to come just around the corner.

...

One morning that spring, I woke up with the sun shining in through my bedroom window. The east-facing window welcomed the early morning rays, a bright light that always brought me back to the reality of the life I was living. Sleeping was my only regular escape from suffering. I rolled over to check my phone. It was 6:30 a.m., time to get up. But why was there a text message from my brother John when he was just across the hall? I opened the text and read words that silenced everything else in my mind: "Dad died this morning."

I read the text again, then checked myself to make sure I wasn't dreaming. I was wide awake. I scrambled to get out of bed and find my brother. John was sitting on his bed with an expressionless look on his face. He told me that our aunt Dana had reached out with the news early that morning, after our father took his final breaths with family surrounding him. He was thirty-nine years old, and he had followed the exact path the doctors had warned him against: His cirrhosis had progressed to a point of no return. For the previous year, his condition had been slowly declining until finally his life withered away.

I stared at my brother. We hadn't seen our dad for a few years, and now it was over. Really over. There would never be another chance for him, for us, or for anyone else in his life to reconnect and repair the breaks in our relationships. That hit hard, and it echoed the hopelessness I felt about everything else in my life. With a house of five, hundreds of kids at school, and dozens of family members around, I should have felt enveloped by support, but instead I felt surrounded by darkness, by walls closing in, and by despair. I stood in John's room staring out the west-facing window at the trees that surrounded the house across the road. The house looked like it was suffocating, emblematic of my life. Tree branches reached down as if they were aiming at the core of the house, ready to collapse the roof and walls. Shadows covered the front of the building, with gaps of light shining through to the peak. Without any more words, I turned as quickly as I could, stormed into my room, and dropped my face into my hands. I wanted to scream, to cry, to explode, but there was nothing in me to come out. The state of depression I'd been in allowed so little feeling through. Life had left me, and I wanted to leave it. I wished, for the first time in a long time, that I was dead. On my knees, crouched over my bed, I wanted to succumb to the belief that my life was over. But I knew that somehow, I had to get myself together and get through the day.

In the days that followed, I bounced between numbness and pain. The trip to Massachusetts for my dad's funeral offered a short respite from daily life, but when I returned to Minnesota, reality struck again. Smoking pot with the small group of buddies I still had would offer a temporary feeling of hope, but when my friends left, I was stuck with my thoughts and those always took me to dark places. I was full of fear, especially of being alone. While a small part of me still cared about others and missed my old friends, those feelings were mostly crowded out by the pain, selfishness, and misery that my life consisted of.

...

One Friday afternoon about a week after my return to Minnesota, I stopped at a buddy's place with my mom. She was there to say hello to a friend and didn't know I was really tagging along for one thing only—some pot. As she headed upstairs, I went down to the cellar. It was a typical unfinished basement, with concrete floors, a few small, thick glass windows near the top of each wall, and a bit of a musty smell and feel. At the bottom of the creaky, wooden stairs, an older friend of mine, Tommy, was sitting in the spot we used to get high. A quick hello and hug connected the two of us. I smelled something different, something like a cleaning solution. I was a bit puzzled, but Tommy was always good to me and fun to hang out with, so I wasn't worried. "Want to try something new?" he asked. I couldn't possibly say no. I couldn't risk any more rejection, and at that vulnerable point, I was willing to try anything to ease some of the pain I was living with. "Sit here and just put your mouth on the pipe; let me do the rest," he instructed.

I sat on the beat-up green couch next to Tommy and followed his direction. He held the pipe to my mouth, held a lighter under it, and began spinning. The smoke quickly filled the end of the pipe, thick and swirling. "When I tell you to, let go, inhale and exhale right away." As soon as he stopped, I did exactly what he said and inhaled and exhaled quickly. The smoke that poured out of my mouth clouded my view and the smell hit me at once. So did the feeling of euphoria. I had an instant sense of satisfaction. All at once, I felt alert, heightened, and full of a certain sense of joy. My entire body tingled, starting in my head and spreading to my toes. Where a moment before I had felt like I was carrying two large tree trunks on my shoulders, suddenly I was floating on that couch. My eyes lit up and it was then that I knew my joy was back.

"How was that?" asked Tommy. I nodded with a big smile and asked for another hit. The second time jolted me even harder—I could feel my body starting to shake and I had to stand up. Tommy laughed. He knew I had just experienced something I'd never forget. He took one more hit and gave me a couple more. I felt more alive than I could ever remember feeling. We each lit a cigarette. Mine tasted and felt different; it was so much more noticeable, tasted better, and was as smooth as any cigarette I had ever smoked. I had no idea what I had just smoked, but I didn't care. I didn't care about anything, and yet I cared about everything at the same time. It felt like a new life had just hit me, one I was never prepared for.

I didn't leave Tommy's side that weekend, as for the first time, methamphetamine powered my life. We hung together, traveling from town to town, staying up all night, playing cards and having fun. The weekend was a bit of a blur, but my feeling of euphoria only grew. Every hit I took felt as good as the first, maybe better. I wasn't afraid of anything. I wasn't depressed. And most of all, I wasn't thinking about everything I had lost. Everything was brighter, lighter, and more fun than before. Before I knew it, Sunday night had arrived and Tommy was bringing me home. My mom had been texting me, upset that I was gone all weekend, wondering what I was doing. I began to worry a bit, but the high I was experiencing made it all okay. Tommy stopped at McDonald's and asked what I wanted, but I wasn't hungry. In fact, I realized I hadn't eaten the entire weekend. Nor, now that I thought about it, had I drunk any-thing. The weekend flew by and never once did I think about food or drink. But Tommy insisted I eat something. He ordered a couple double cheeseburgers and a soda.

On the fifteen-mile drive down country roads, I forced myself to open the burger and start eating it. I took the first bite and immediately felt an intense pain in my mouth. With every chew of that first bite, it felt like I was chomping down on a bunch of skinny razor blades. As pain pierced the inside of my mouth, my gums, and my tongue, those first few bites told me something was terribly wrong. I asked Tommy about it. He simply said I needed to keep eating, that my body was probably in shock because I hadn't eaten for two full days. The bites got a little easier, but I'll never forget the pain I was in. I went from a state of the highest euphoria to a state of deep pain, and fast. I began to crash a bit, feeling like I needed sleep. We pulled into my driveway and Tommy said goodbye. "Let's talk tomorrow," I insisted. I thanked him for a wonderful weekend and hopped out of his baby-blue Oldsmobile. As the headlights backed away, down the part-gravel, part-grass driveway, I knew he was going to be an integral part of my bounce back from my downfall in life.

I walked inside and reassured my mom that I had been staying with Tommy and everything was okay. But she knew something was up and scolded me for being out of touch all weekend. I apologized and headed straight for my room. As I lay there in bed, staring at the ceiling in the dark, the moon pouring a little light in, all I could think about was when I could have an experience like that again. It had to be soon, no doubt. I knew I had something that would take all the pain away now. And that was all the comfort I needed. My eyelids became too heavy to hold open. Fighting the feeling of coming down, I drifted away into the rest that my body so desperately needed.

....

As my junior year came to an end, methamphetamine, prescription opiates and stimulants, alcohol, and marijuana—in that order—became my greatest tools to cope with the pain in my life. Summertime brought a little relief from school and everything it reminded me of. With drugs and alcohol at the center of every day, my relationships began to deteriorate, especially at home. I couldn't get along with my mom, and of course I thought everything was her fault. One day when the constant arguing had gotten to be too much, I took off and stayed with Tommy and his roommate uptown. We partied a ton that summer and I settled into a new life with new friends, a new place to live, and close to no responsibilities. I had no parent to answer to, no job, no vehicle, and no money. I relied heavily on everyone around me. That was always the trade-off—no responsibility meant no resources. But that was okay, because it was how I grew up and was something I was used to. Always having to ask for cigarettes, hits of drugs, drinks, and even food, though, began to contribute to my growing sense of unworthiness.

The only thing that drew me back to school that fall was the promise of playing football. Football provided a release from life's stressors that only the strongest drugs could match, and it was one of the only things that gave me hope from day to day. After my injury, then time spent on the bench due to failing grades and getting busted drinking and driving, my senior year was an opportunity to finally start on our varsity team and not split time with anyone else. Coach Stork, our head coach, wasn't too pleased with the fact that I'd never made it to the weight room over the summer, but he allowed me a starting spot on the team anyway.

Coach Stork was tall and wide, with light brown hair that had a tint of blond in the summer. He towered over all of us and had a personality to match. As we took the field before our first game, he grabbed me on each side of my helmet and said, "Go have a year, Lennox!" I carried the ball five times that game, scoring two touchdowns and a two-point conversion and running for a total of seventy-two yards. We destroyed that team, so I was out of the game by halftime, having gotten a small taste of what that field would do for me that year. We played each Friday, and every week, I looked increasingly forward to the games. All my old friends played, too, and while they wouldn't even acknowledge me at school, those few hours each week brought us all together and felt like a return to the old days. My success also meant I was constantly in the spotlight, featured as the player of the week on local radio and TV stations, newspapers, and more. Football stardom brought worth to my life once again, and it gave me a reason to get up each day. Our team had the best season in recent memory, maybe ever. But unfortunately, this shining period would turn out to be the last time for a long while that I felt genuinely excited about life.

As the season wrapped up, so did my reason to be in school. I dropped out later that fall. With no ability to contribute to Tommy and his roommate, I was asked to leave their home, and soon I had lost everything. I had no job, no home, no money, and worst of all, no purpose.

My life turned dark quickly. Most days I'd have to ask for food, water, and a couch to sleep on. I had just a few friends, all of whom hesitated to share much with me. I was the mooch of the town, and knowing that crushed my self-worth and ego. Thankfully, one of my few remaining friends, Rob, introduced me to an out-of-town girl he had been dating on and off for a while. I remember standing on the sidewalk when they pulled up. She sat in the driver's seat, with beautiful blond hair down to her shoulder blades. She had bright green eyes and an irresistible smile to match. The look she gave me struck me as strange, considering she was dating my friend. But as it turned out, they weren't dating, just friends, and later

# I had no job, no home, no money, and worst of all, no purpose.

that same night she texted me to ask if I'd like to hang out sometime. I finally felt like I had caught a break. Chasity had everything I didn't—a car, a home, money, food, and what seemed like a sense of happiness. It was a bonus that she looked stunning. She asked when we could hang out, and with an empty schedule and nothing else in my life, I told her the next day worked for me. She agreed to pick me up.

That next evening turned into a relationship, a home, and a sense of security I desperately needed. While the truth was that we couldn't seem to get along after day three, my need for a place to live outweighed the fighting and discomfort of the relationship. Chasity's parents allowed me to stay with her in the home they had bought for her until I found a place. They soon made it clear that my permanent presence in her home wasn't part of the plan.

Chasity babysat for a family with several foster kids, and one afternoon we stopped by their home so she could introduce me. Their house was tucked away in a quiet neighborhood on the south end of Waseca, and it had a main level and a finished basement. It was a late fall afternoon, and the sun was shin-ing down from the west side of the house as we walked up the driveway to the side door. Chasity told me that the family had their own kids, but they had also taken care of dozens

> For awhile, living in the Hoy Family's home brought a sense of belonging, even of being needed.

and dozens of others over the years. At the time, they had a particularly challenging threesome of kids—a pair of twins about six months old, as well as a toddler—who had been born as "meth babies." As a result, all three had delayed cognitive abilities, emotional instability, and other physical issues.

The Hoy family also ran an in-home daycare, so when the side door opened, the peace of the fall afternoon quickly faded. There were kids everywhere. To the right was a wide-open, very large living area, and to the left, an open kitchen and dining area. Cathy welcomed us in and introduced herself. She was warm and energetic, a short woman with shoulder-length wavy brown hair and a strong presence. It was easy to see she was the center of everything in that house. Her husband, Devin, arrived home from his construction job shortly after, and he struck me as his wife's opposite. Smaller in stature, with a short crew cut that was always covered by a baseball cap, he was much quieter than Cathy.

As Chasity and I spent more time at the Hoy residence, they learned about my situation. When they discovered I needed a place to stay they offered up their basement. My friend Rob, the one who had introduced me to Chasity, had lived there previously, and he was also in need of a structured environment again. So I agreed to move into the basement with Rob, where we shared space and had beds not far from each other.

Though their home was always full of kids coming and going, there was a peace about the Hoy house and that family. They supported me getting back into my old school, where I would have to work for a few weeks to get caught up on the couple of months I had missed. Though it still felt like a nightmare seeing my old group fade further and further away, I knew I was lucky to be back at all. The drugs helped, too. Meth and prescription stimulants always helped me to feel a little more okay with life. Everything just felt easier on stimulants, like life was the way it was supposed to be. But on the off days, life was so hard. When I came off the drugs, I felt tired, anxious, dreadful, and heavy. Going to school and getting through even one class was a chore.

For a while, living in the Hoy family's home brought a sense of belonging, even of being needed. I helped with the kids as much as I could. More than anything about my time there, I remember how deeply connected I felt to the kids they were fostering, the ones born to meth-addicted parents. I developed an especially close relationship to one of the young twins. Maya was the more even-tempered of the two, with less crying and screaming, and she was my little buddy. I watched her, held her, and got close enough to her that she felt like a sibling of my own. Ironically, I couldn't look at her situation and truly grasp the gravity of what meth could do to a human. I watched how the twins cried for no reason, had a hard time settling down, and didn't sleep that well, and it gave a little insight into the danger of the drug. But I was deep into the beginning of a serious addiction to meth, and no force or example was going to stop that power.

The Hoy family had offered me shelter, food, guidance, education, and financial support, and soon they made it clear that they wanted to help with this "problem" that was becoming more apparent to those around me. Chasity and her parents were aware of it, too, and as a result my relationship with her had begun to fall apart. The Hoys began talking openly about addiction and the problems they saw in my life. With the right blend of compassion and frankness, they made it clear they wanted me to address my drug problem. The walls were closing in again, and I couldn't handle being faced with responsibility for the difficulties in my life. So I did what I always did best— ran. In the middle of the night, I convinced Rob to sneak out the side door with me and off into the night we went.

My mom still had our house in New Richland, but at the time she was living with her fiancé a few towns over, so I talked her into letting us crash at her New Richland place for a bit. She hesitantly agreed, but she made it clear that the place was to be kept up and treated nicely. For a few weeks we partied, had fun, and did a lot of drugs in that home. Then came the fateful day that my mom visited.

Knowing she would be back soon, we had spent a frenzied, meth-fueled day cleaning intensely, even scrubbing the carpets. I was in school the next day when I saw a missed call and voice mail from my mom. I knew she must have called with a message of gratitude, thrilled with the cleanliness of the place. But I was wrong. It turned out someone had taken a bunch of her saved change, and she was irate about it. She had left me a long, disappointed, angry message, in which she let me know she had changed the locks and I'd never be allowed there again. I was crushed . . . and worse, I had no idea where to go. I had screwed over the foster family, had just told Chasity I never wanted to see her again, and had now been given the boot from my mom's place. It was the last half of my senior year of high school, and I was off to the streets. Again.

"

# RUNNING AWAY FROM YOUR PROBLEM IS A RACE YOU'LL NEVER WIN.

UNKNOWN

CHAPTER 6

# ON THE RUN

It was about 11 p.m. on a late winter night and everyone was starting to go in for the night in New Richland. I parted ways with a few people at the park on the main street with one goal: to find a warm place to sleep. The temperature was about forty degrees and falling. I could see my breath on every exhale, and the cold, crisp air began to make my extremities numb. My nose and ears were rosy red. While the air was refreshing, I knew I couldn't spend the night out there. No coat and no gloves meant I needed some cover. I looked into the night sky and thought about my next move. I headed across town to a familiar road—the one I used to live on. It was close to midnight by then, and the dead-end road was lit up by a handful of streetlights. In one of the darker stretches in front of my buddy Dustin's house, I saw his dad's baby-blue car parked on the street. A warmer night of sleep was dependent on one of its doors being open. I walked up to the rear passenger door, took a glance around at all the houses to make sure no one was watching, and pulled the handle. It opened. I quickly snuck in, shut the door, and waited for the interior light to dim. As darkness settled in, I laid on my back and stared at the roof of the house the car was in front of. I tossed and turned all night, startled by every sound I heard and doing my best to stay as warm as I could. At about 4 a.m., worried I'd fall asleep again and miss the 5 a.m. deadline when Dustin's dad would have to leave for work, I crept out of the car. Cold, tired, and full of anxiety, I headed back uptown to get ready for another day to start.

At night, all my other troubles would fade away as I focused on meeting the basic human need of shelter. But as the sun began to rise, all those other problems quickly returned. I was eighteen, without a home, a car, a job, money, and often food. Those were the kind of problems that would normally dominate a person's thinking, but for me the first and only goal was to find a way to quiet all that anxiety with a fix of drugs or alcohol. I didn't really care which it was, I only cared about drowning out my painful reality. Yet again, Dustin unknowingly came to the rescue. He and I used to run to his grandma's house and snag a few shots of her vodka, then replace it with water to avoid setting off any alarms. As soon as it hit 8 a.m., I knew she would be off to work, and she lived just four blocks from where I had rested the night before, about halfway down another dead-end road. I walked down the driveway to the backyard. Watching carefully for anyone who might be in their yards, I snuck in through the back door.

The kitchen was silent, with dated fixtures, decades-old wallpaper, and paper-thin carpet that looked soiled and worn. Light shone in through the windows. I had to get in and out quickly, as all those windows made me feel incredibly exposed. Under the sink was the warm bottle of cheap vodka. Adrenaline and a calming relief filled me equally. I knew, even before I had drunk any, that I'd feel better soon. I took three of the biggest swigs I could, poured some into an empty bottle she had, replaced the vodka with water from the faucet, and exited through the back door. The garage was on the right, and I walked along it through the backyard, up the hill, and onto the train tracks, never looking back. I strolled down the tracks and over to the park, where I took a seat at the bottom of a hill. I gulped a few more sips from the bottle of warm vodka and let it settle in. The day was going to be okay.

With my biggest problem temporarily resolved, I next turned to finding food, as I hadn't eaten since early the prior day. I scoured the ground as I walked through the park and up the main street, looking for lost change. I found a quarter—more than enough to get a snack at the local grocery store. I bought a bag of ramen noodles and walked back to the park, where I crushed the noodles, added the seasoning, and ate them like a bag of chips. That was how I spent the last couple months of my senior year: searching for places to sleep by night, stealing and mooching whatever alcohol and drugs I could, and rounding up any food I could by day, attending school about half of the time. Yet despite the circumstances, I never thought about my life as troubled—I didn't have time. I was too focused on solving the immediate issues in front of me each day to think about my problems or how to find a way out. But that would all change when I discovered my problems weren't mine alone.

Although I had told Chasity I never wanted to see her again, not long after she asked to see me in person because she had some news. I agreed, and almost immediately, with tears in her eyes, she told me she was pregnant. My first thought was, *This is a lie.* She had always told me she couldn't get pregnant, and I suspected ulterior motives, so I called what I thought was her bluff and asked her to leave. I was done listening to her. She went on her way, but eventually some ultrasound pictures, the rumblings around the community, and her growing size made it apparent she wasn't lying. I was in disbelief. Having a child was the last thing I felt able to deal with. I couldn't get my own life straight, and I knew I had no business being responsible for another human. I did everything I could to drown out my fear and forget it was happening. Chasity and I fought and, in a drunken stupor one night after an argument, I did some damage to her car. Her father called me and told me that if I didn't fix it, they'd be pressing charges, but I ignored him and did what I did best in any conflict—I ran.

On a Sunday night later that spring, I found out there was a warrant for my arrest because I had missed a presentence investigation related to the criminal property damage charges. I had never received the notice because the court had sent it to my mom's. I tried to build up the courage to approach the police in that small town, wearing the warrant like a badge of honor as I proudly shared with my friends that I'd be turning myself in. I approached the cop on duty, who was parked on Main Street, and told him I was willingly surrendering myself. Apparently, he didn't want to work late that night, so he told me I could deal with it the next day and went on his way. Later that week, I turned myself in to the county jail. I thought they'd let me back out after clearing the air, but I was wrong. They told me I'd be staying for a bit and would need to take a urinalysis test for drugs in my system. I had been up for a couple days doing meth and knew that test wouldn't work in my favor. I argued with everyone that testing would do nothing to show what my state of mind had been on the night of the crime, but they didn't budge, and after hours of wearing myself down, I needed some water and a bathroom break. I agreed to pee in the cup if they'd let me go to my cell and sleep. Coach Stork, who had heard what was going on, had driven a half hour to have a much-needed conversation with me, but I angrily refused his visit and opted for sleep instead. The next few days in jail went slower than any I had ever had. I was brought to see the judge, who expressed concerns about my lifestyle. In anger, I criticized him for making judgments about my life without knowing me—not a good idea, as he ordered me to sit a few more nights in jail.

After my release, I somehow managed to finish the school year and walk across the stage with a signed diploma. Then I met with my probation officer and convinced her to let me move to Massachusetts. I had to get out of town. I was tired of running, bouncing around, and experiencing food and shelter insecurity, and I knew I would have a place to stay with my uncle if I moved there. But to persuade my probation officer, I simply told her, "If you hung out with the people I hang out with, you'd understand why I do drugs." Maybe out of pity, or maybe because she didn't want to deal with me, she ordered me to do an evaluation upon my arrival in Massachusetts and granted my request.

My uncle Wayne offered me a bed in the basement of his house in Springfield, Massachusetts. Wayne was my dad's younger brother. He lived in a green, two-story house down a quiet road. Finally, I again had shelter, food, and a little support. My uncle's ex-girlfriend still lived with him, along with their four kids, who ranged in ages from five to eighteen. Though the house was full of people, conflict, and continuous noise, the basement was a peaceful escape. I had my own bed, my own room, and a sense of belonging. I scheduled the evaluation with a new probation officer. He gave me an intelligence test, and after I showed I could count backward from a hundred by seven in seconds, he sent me on my way with no restrictions. I was free to do whatever I wanted and was no longer on probation with any state or county. What a relief it was to know that my drug and alcohol use could continue.

In Springfield, I spent a lot of time with another uncle, Todd. He was my mom's brother, and he supported me as much as possible. He had paid for my ticket to Massachusetts, and he even bought a cheap van and put it in my name. Uncle Todd was always one of the most generous people in my life. He had taken care of me and my brother as kids, especially after my mom divorced, and we always got excited when we knew he was coming to visit. He drove hazardous material around the country in his van for a living and would stop to see us on his way through, most of the time for a week or so. The support I got from him and the time we spent together that summer changed the trajectory of my life—for a while, at least.

Todd picked me up from Uncle Wayne's shortly after I arrived in Massachusetts and drove us down to Westfield, a town about thirty minutes from Springfield, where his friend Tom lived. We pulled his white van into the driveway, wire fence lining the left side and the house on the right. The driveway opened into a large paved area with a garage on the right past the house, and a basketball hoop hanging from the first stall. The property was surrounded by trees and sat in a quiet neighborhood. It was a warm summer afternoon, and Tom stood waiting for us in his usual uniform—jean shorts cut off about halfway up his thigh, no shirt, and sandals, his shaggy, dark brown hair curling around his ears. He stood with a cigarette in his mouth, eyes a bit glossy, and a big smile on his face. "Todd!" he shrieked in his raspy, high-pitched voice. Tom was a laid-back guy who was quick with a joke, and he lived with his girlfriend and her two kids. Over the next two months, I began to spend a lot of time with them. I learned that Tom had been an alcoholic earlier in life, but he had managed to kick that habit—though it quickly became clear that he had simply replaced it with pot. His girlfriend, on the other hand, still liked to drink. They were a generous couple, and gladly offered me anything I could ask for: food, drink, pot, cigarettes, and more.

At Tom's house, I began to find ways of rationalizing my addiction. Being with my dad's family after his death was a strong reminder that drinking was a problem in my life, so at first, I opted for marijuana smoking with Tom. Smoking was fun, relaxing, and seemingly trouble-free, but it got boring after a while, so I convinced myself drinking was the more reasonable option. After all, marijuana was illegal at the time.

When drinking, in turn, brought me to my knees, it was easy to convince myself that marijuana was a safer choice, because at least it wouldn't kill me like alcohol. Back and forth I went from one chemical to the other. It was better than my Minnesota life, I thought, because at least I was staying away from the hard drugs. Of course, in reality, that was more a result of not having any connections than it was a conscious choice. But for the first time in a long while, life felt like it was acceptable again. I was out of trouble, away from hard drugs, and had even landed a job working a food booth at a local fair. It was only a three-week gig, but it was one of the few jobs I'd ever had and I was working enough hours to save a few bucks. I knew I'd need that money, with the imminent birth of my son. He was due sometime in October, and as my mind cleared up just a bit, I knew I had to be there for him. I promised myself I would never let him experience the kind of loss I had endured. I was going to break the cycle. My son was going to have a life worth living, and I was going to have something, or more importantly, someone else to live for. That felt good. Life felt good. I had finally found a sense of purpose.

I woke up one early October day and prepared for the day as usual—smoked a cigarette, brushed my teeth, and looked for a quick bite to eat. I had stopped working after the fair ended, and I had been spending time with family while waiting for the call I knew was coming from Minnesota. Later that day, I received a text from Chasity that she was likely going to the hospital in the next day or so. I was struck with anxiety and all kinds of thoughts about what was next. I didn't have much time. I quickly told my uncle, my grandpa, and my other family members that I had to get back for my son's birth. There was a sense of pride and excitement in telling everyone my child was on his way. The next day, I packed up my belongings and loaded up the purple Dodge Caravan my uncle had given me. Before I left, I headed down to Westfield and gave away my bag of pot. I knew I had a new life to build in Minnesota as a father.

A little more than twenty-four hours later, I arrived in Minnesota with a new sense of self-worth. I had put on twenty to thirty pounds of weight, had a van to my name, and had a new outlook thanks to the excitement of becoming a father. It was a Friday evening, and when I arrived in New Richland I found a few old friends preparing for a party in the backyard. They were waiting for a couple kegs of beer to arrive, but I didn't intend to drink. I had a bigger intention that day—to be with my son. Chasity was in the hospital by the time I arrived, so I said a quick hello to my friends, then took off for the hospital in a nearby town. My friend Dustin, seemingly just as excited as I was to see a new child arrive in the world, offered to ride with me, and I welcomed the company, knowing it would be awkward to see Chasity and her family again.

I walked into the hospital full of anxiety, fear, and excitement, as well as a level of shame and guilt over having walked away from Chasity while she was in the middle of her pregnancy. But I knew getting out of town had been the best thing for me. I stepped up to the front desk and informed the staff member we were there to see my son and his mother. She pointed the way, and as I walked down the hall, I wondered what it would feel like to see him. What would my son look like? How would everyone else react to my being there? What was life going to look like with a child? The moment of truth came as I turned the corner into the room.

The hospital room was quite large, with lights everywhere compensating for the darkness that was developing outside. To the right, there were chairs, hospital staff, and all kinds of medical supplies. Behind the bed, near the window, stood Chasity's mom and stepdad, Tracy and John. Tracy was short and petite, with dyed blond hair reaching down just past her shoulders. John was on the shorter side, too, with glasses and a graying crew cut. He was an optometrist, and Tracy was an employee at his office. They did well in life. They had always been civil to me, but I never felt like they understood my life or where I came from, and it had always blocked me from feeling any real connection with them. As I entered the room, they smiled and asked how I was, then watched in anticipation to see how my interaction with Chasity would unfold.

Straight ahead on the bed, Chasity lay holding our son, Aiden. She had had a rough go with the birth and looked like she was suffering, but her smile was beautiful as she stared down at him. After a few seconds of deafening silence, she quietly asked the question I was waiting to hear: "Do you want to hold him?" Of course I did. I stepped up to the bedside and with shaking arms and legs, transferred the tiny boy from her arms to mine. I cradled him tightly and stared into his face. I felt full of fear and uncertainty, but his face was full of innocence. His eyes were closed and his head was full of greasy dark brown hair. His body was wrapped in two blankets, making him feel like a little heater. I watched his chest rise and fall subtly and quickly with each breath he took. I held him for a while, rocking him back and forth and hoping he wouldn't wake up. He was sleeping so peacefully. Awe set in. This little body was partly a creation of mine. I'd heard many stories of instantaneous love during that first hold, but my experience was different. I was still so full of uncertainty, discomfort, and fear that I couldn't really feel the effect I had heard about from so many other new parents. But as I began to settle down and take in the moment, I knew I had a purpose and a mission with this boy of mine. Caring for him was something I knew needed to be taken seriously.

I left knowing that it was time to make sure my life was clean and together. But when I arrived at my friends' party, it didn't take long for them to convince me that it was a night to party. I was a father! Of course that called for celebration. Though I knew I needed to change my ways, it wasn't long before I found myself doing keg stands, slamming beer, and cheering with some of my old friends. I drank to oblivion that night, and the next morning, I drove again to see my son, which I had committed to doing every single day.

I spent the next several weeks sleeping in my van, waking up and driving to see Aiden, then finding friends later in the day to have a few drinks with. I was still drinking almost every day, but had managed to kick all the drugs, and I had landed a job at an express oil-change shop in Waseca. It wasn't the most glamorous job and most days I stared at the clock waiting to get out of there, but it brought a brief period of stability and some income to my life. Eventually I caught wind that Chasity was in a new relationship, and it terrified me to think some other guy was around my newborn son and might replace me.

I wondered if Chasity and I could have a better relationship without drugs running my life. We began to work things out and decided to give it another shot. I moved in with Chasity and tried to learn how to take responsibility, but it was hard to be eighteen and be a parent. I knew I had to cut down on my drinking, at least during the week, but I was miserable and cranky. All my friends were partying and having fun, and I was home tending to a girlfriend and child. Addiction had a strong grip on me, and staying sober even for a few days was painful. When I was able to drink on weekends, I drank heavily.

One night in 2006, only about six months after I had moved in with Chasity, I was picked up for drunk driving. I had just purchased a car and was driving home after a night of beers at a friend's place. I was pulled over one block from home with both my taillights out. I lost my license, had to pay a bunch of money in fines and fees, and this created more strain in many of my relationships. At just nineteen years old, I had been in and out of jail several times, leaving behind a trail of shame and embarrassment, and I hardly realized addiction was slowly taking any last chances of a successful life away. Sadly, without a responsible and consistent father, my son was suffering the most, but I couldn't see or recognize that. I was in a self-seeking state of mind, always looking to feed the addiction and stop the pain.

Eventually, after enough fights and misery, I decided to walk away from my relationship with Chasity and move in with a coworker. I was working in construction, which for me meant a lot of drinking and late nights, and Chasity told me I wouldn't be allowed to see Aiden with the way I was living. My relationship with my son slowly faded, and with it went any sense of purpose and meaning in my life. I was living to drink and drinking to live. My anxiety grew greater and greater by the day, and my only escape was to drink more. I still managed to keep away from drugs, but alcohol had a strong grip on my life. After a drunken night of fighting, I shattered the window of my roommate's car and was given the boot from that home. I had nowhere else to go.

For the next couple years, I bounced around between short-term jobs and places to stay. I tried to mend the relationship with my mom, who offered me a room in the basement of the home she was sharing with her fiancé. I enrolled in college multiple times but never actually started school, and I never lasted more than a few months at a job. My drinking continued to progress, and drugs slowly came back into the picture. I reconnected with my cousin Scott, who I had grown up idolizing and who lived in the same town as my mom. Scott was a few years older than me. When I was little, he had dragged me along to all the sports he played and taught me a lot. He had gone away for a few years and cleaned up his life after a bout with drugs and alcohol. He moved back to the area, where he began drinking again, though he seemed to be managing his life well. We dabbled in some drugs, partied all the time, and worked hard during the week. Eventually, I landed a job working in a machine shop and a room in an apartment my older brother, John, had rented and later vacated.

Though I struggled to consciously think about the son I had left behind, I felt the guilt inside. Everything I had ever promised not to be as a father, I was. Every now and then I'd think about that poor little boy. But I couldn't stay in that thought long, and I would quickly seek an escape through more drugs and alcohol. The machine shop gig was a decent-paying job, so after I had received a few regular paychecks, hard partying became an every-weekend occurrence. And that's where the serious trouble began.

# " 

# LOSING YOUR LIFE IS NOT THE WORST THING THAT CAN HAPPEN. THE WORST THING IS TO LOSE YOUR REASON FOR LIVING.

JO NESBO

# CHAPTER 7

# THE BEGINNING OF THE END

Name: LENNOX, JASO

Booking Date    4/12/2008 21:12

LENNOX, JASON ANTHONY

4/12/2008 21:12

It was a Thursday night in late spring, a season that always came with a renewed energy in Minnesota. Thursday night meant Thirsty Thursday. I called up my buddy Ryan, a former coworker who lived in Hayfield, a town about fifteen minutes away. Like me, Ryan had a medium build, about five feet, ten inches. He had short, dark brown hair, and a personality that couldn't go unnoticed. He drove a new white Mustang that was loud, fast, and powerful. I looked up to him in some ways. His house was a bachelor pad if ever I saw one, with more beer than food, a sink full of dishes, and mismatching furniture all over the place. I was the first guest to arrive, and he met me with a firm handshake, a shoulder tap, and most importantly, an ice-cold can of beer. We enjoyed a couple beers together before he told me he had something else to share. He pulled

71

out a bag of white powder—cocaine. I'd never done drugs with him, and it caught me off guard. Cocaine wasn't as strong as meth, I reasoned, but it wasn't as harmful, either. We snorted a few lines together. The fine, white powder came up through the rolled-up dollar bill fast and hard, burning my nose and the entire passage down to my throat. While it was a bit painful to take in, it provided a euphoria and sense of relief many other things could not. It lit a fire inside me. Ryan was my best friend that night. We quickly shifted the party back downstairs to the kitchen, where we took a few shots of liquor and continued slamming cans of beer, welcoming everyone who came through with happiness and excitement. There was no time for sleep that night.

I called in to work the next day and told them I wasn't feeling well, but it seemed like they knew better. I quickly drowned out that worry with another drink. I drank all day and connected with a couple old buddies to continue the party that night. The night quickly turned into a blur as I drank shot after shot and beer after beer. I was in a true state of oblivion. When I woke up the next morning on a couch in the living room of some old acquaintances, I couldn't remember much. I looked out the patio door to see the sun rising over the horizon. It was so bright, and I had a headache from hell. My head was pounding, my body seemed half dead, and I felt like I could throw up right there. No one else was up, so I scrambled through the kitchen to find something to take the pain away. Most people in pain would run from its cause and try to recover, but not me—when the pain came, I sought more of the thing that had caused it. I took a quick couple shots of vodka and sat back down. I was so far from settled, full of unease and discomfort. As I sat on the sectional couch with my hands in my lap, I could only think of one thing—getting rid of that pounding pain. I fell back asleep briefly and woke to the sound of my friends chatting. We decided to go uptown for breakfast to the local bar and grill, one of the few hot spots in that town of a few hundred. While everyone else ordered food, I ordered a bloody Mary. I asked anyone if they had ibuprofen, and someone jokingly responded with an offer of a couple opiate prescription pills: "That will take all your pain away." Yeah, it sure would. I quickly and gladly accepted the offer and popped a couple at once, washing them down with the bloody Mary before ordering another. Then another. Suddenly, all the pain was gone. Life was all I ever hoped it could be. I was free, relaxed, pain-free, worry-free, and comfortable in my own skin; so opposite to the normal feelings I experienced every day. I drifted away to a place of solace and restfulness. I closed my eyes and faded into oblivion—first figuratively, and then, at some point, literally.

The next day, I woke up on a thin, plastic mattress. As my eyes opened, the first thing I experienced was pain. The bright light shining from the ceiling was hard to look at. My head felt like a hammer had been tapping it all night. I rolled to my left and sat up. After a minute of coming to a full state of consciousness, I realized where I was: back in jail, a place I had managed to avoid for the past couple years. I looked at the gray walls in front of me, the sun shining through the square window high on the wall to the right, then to my left at the metal door with a two-foot-wide window near the top. I stood up and walked to the door. Through the window, I could see a balding corrections officer sitting at the center desk. I knocked on the window and he stood. He was tall and round near the waist, and as he approached, I could see his belt held all kinds of little gadgets, including a Taser, handcuffs, and a walkie-talkie. He came around the corner of the enclosed sitting area, all his keys clanking against each other and ringing throughout the entire pod, and stood in front of the door. "Why am I here?" I asked. "Hold on," he said. He walked back around to the desk and picked up some pieces of paper, which he slid through a slot in the door. "This will tell you everything you need to know."

I sat down on the bed and began to read with an over-whelming anxiety. With every word, reading got harder and harder. The two most important lines were:

CHARGE: POSSESSION OF CONTROLLED SUBSTANCES, FELONY

PUNISHMENT: UP TO FIVE YEARS IN PRISON

As I read the narrative, bits and pieces of the prior day started to come back to me. I remembered arriving at the Eagles Club with my roommate Bart. Bart and I had a long history, much of which was bad, but we'd recently mended our relationship and moved in together. We strolled through the building, chatting with anyone we knew. I grabbed another drink and began messaging contacts in my phone, looking for more cocaine. I knew I'd need a pick-me-up to make it through that night. Bart said he had a connection and would get more for us, but I lost track of him, and when I called him a little later, it was clear he had left without me and was out doing some more drugs with a few others. Drunk and craving my next high, I let some choice words fly at Bart, then sat down to take a breather on a bench in the entryway, full of liquor, pills, and the remnants of stimulants from a couple nights prior. I faded on that bench, waiting for someone to miraculously deliver me more drugs. When I woke up, I was lying down and staring into the eyes of two police officers. One of them was bent over me, taking my pulse and checking to make sure I was breathing. I sat up quickly and saw a crowd watching with interest. The police officers asked me to stand, and they explained I was under arrest for possession of drugs. Enraged, I told them to let me go, insisting that I didn't have any drugs in my possession. They showed me a few bags with small amounts of powder in them.

"Those are not mine," I pleaded loudly. "Please, Officer, let me go," I begged again. They walked me outside. I asked for a cigarette, a request they denied, and I continued to argue my case outside in front of the police SUV. They showed me my face in the mirror, and I saw that the right side was covered with black marker others had used to write on me after I'd passed out on the couch. "See?" I exclaimed. "I was clearly messed with and framed!" When it became clear they weren't going to let me go or give in to my begging for a cigarette, I became combative, shouting expletives at the officers and hurting my cause even more. During the entire trip to jail and throughout the intake process, I continued to deny any wrongdoing and blamed everyone else, including the arresting officers, for the bad situation I had found myself in. It wasn't my fault. It never was. Anger replaced oblivion for a short time until, exhausted and beaten down again, I finally fell asleep in my cell.

Now wide awake, I stood back up and tightly grasped my hair, then dropped my head and began pacing. The cell was about six by nine, which didn't leave much room for pacing. As I passed the metal sink attached to the wall, I saw myself in the mirror. My face looked like a balloon, with remnants of black marker around my eye and down my right cheek. I stood there in disbelief, disgust, and despair. I thought about all the people who had watched as the police woke me up and took me away, about the people who had made a mockery of my face with marker, all the people who had seen the disgrace my life had turned into. Looking myself in the face was hard to do. It was almost as if I were looking at another being that inhabited my body. I knew the person I saw was not the person I was meant to be.

For the first time in a long time, I stopped to think about where my life was, how it had progressed over the past few years, and what my future held. I had hardly even realized it as I walked away from my son, lost my vehicle, and picked up some more criminal charges. I blurred it all out with as many drinks and drugs as I could find. Now, locked up on one of the most embarrassing weekends of my life, I had to face the music. The only question was, what would the music be? I turned my attention back to the paperwork, where the words practically jumped off the page—*up to five years in prison.* Five years. It must have been a mistake. After all, I hardly had enough for one small fix of coke. I asked the guard if the five-year sentence was realistic, and he told me he wasn't allowed to discuss that with me. I was let out for an hour that day, and in that time, I connected with another inmate who had recently been locked up. I brought my intake paperwork with me and asked him the million-dollar question: "Can they actually lock me up for five years?" He replied, "I've seen people get caught with less and go away for just as long." That statement pierced right through me. I felt like I was going to throw up. I ran back to my cell, where I crouched over the toilet and waited. But nothing came. Instead, a few tears started rolling down my face. I grabbed my head, squeezing hard to try and let out the anger and frustration inside. I screamed internally. How could this have happened to me? My questions soon turned to self-pity, pity turned to anger, and anger turned into a restlessness I couldn't shake. I could barely sleep, and I continued to pace for much of that day and night.

The next morning was a Monday, and I was scheduled to see the judge. In the past I had approached judges with a cocky attitude, a feeling of invincibility, and a smart response always at the ready, but this time was different. Much different. When the corrections officer called, "Lennox, time to go" over my intercom, I jumped up, pulled on my orange jumpsuit, and zipped it from bottom to top. I flipped on my matching orange sandals and walked out the door. I was handcuffed and led to a transport van with cages all around the back end. When we arrived at the courthouse, I stepped out of the vehicle with my head down, shame and remorse in my heart, hoping no one would see me there. Inside, the judge made quick work of my appearance.

"Mr. Lennox, I'm going to release you on your own recognizance, meaning you don't need bail money, but you need to refrain from any drug or alcohol use, stay out of bars, and keep yourself out of trouble. We'll have another court date in a couple months."

My relief was immeasurable. I thanked the judge, promised better ways, and turned back to the transporting officer. Back at the detention center, they took an hour or so to process paperwork and get me my street clothes back, and then just like that, I was free, at least for the moment. They escorted me to the front desk and said, "Here you go—the doors are right over there." I couldn't get through them fast enough.

**The tricky thing about addiction is that it can simply take over in certain moments, without a person having any real awareness of it happening.**

I walked out into the warming April air, sun shining down and a slight breeze bringing the smell of freshly cut grass. I cut across the parking lot and began my journey back to town. It was about two miles to get to the closest phone, where I'd need to call for a ride. I walked along the highway, passing the college I had signed up for and dropped out of within days, the industrial park where I'd worked at a factory for just a few weeks on a couple occasions, and over the busiest interstate in Minnesota. I felt an overwhelming sense of fear, remorse, and shame. I knew that everyone driving by saw me and certainly knew that I was coming from that detention center. Not to mention the hundreds of people who must have seen me passed out on the bench in the club lobby. I later saw that the local newspaper had blasted my intake story. I was the laughingstock of the town and was afraid to encounter or talk to anyone. And worst of all, it looked like prison was in my future.

For perhaps the first time since I had started using and drinking, I knew it was really time to quit. On that Monday afternoon walk, as I crossed over the interstate on the bridge above, I promised myself I was done. I knew I faced some serious trouble and I couldn't control that, but I could control never drinking or using again. It was the easiest decision I could ever make. I found a pay phone and scrounged up thirty-five cents to call my roommate, the one who had left me at the Eagles Club two days prior. He picked me up a half hour later and we escaped back to the apartment we shared. There, full of shame, I knew I needed to fabricate the right story. I convinced my roommate that someone must have drugged me, planted drugs on me, and left me to be found. That was the story we'd run with.

One of the trickiest things about addiction is that it can simply take over in certain moments, without a person having any real awareness of it happening. Just hours after being released from jail, without a single thought about the promises I had just made to myself, I was getting high and drunk with the same people at the same places. Inexplicably, one of my first true desires and attempts to get sober disappeared without any conscious decision or thought. It was the beginning of a period of insanity I'd never have believed possible. While I didn't see it at the time, I was experiencing the true feeling of powerlessness that some recovery programs claim is at the core of drug and alcohol addictions. I had no power to stop myself from drinking or drugging, and it was clear that even outside powers—the judge and the law—were not going to stop me.

I was scheduled to be sentenced later that fall, but as I did so often, I failed to show up for court. I had been laid off from work and was staying back in the town I had spent my high school years in, New Richland, with my mom, who had recently moved back. I couldn't stay sober long enough to get to court. Instead, I spent months inside the garage that had brought me so many fun memories in the past. Each morning, I'd hide in the darkness for as long as I could, only coming out into the daylight when I needed to track down drugs and alcohol, or when I had enough drugs and alcohol in my system to show my face to the world.

One weekend while I was staying with my buddy Michael, I got so drunk and emotional that I called the cops and let them know who I was and where I was. With active warrants, the cops told me they'd be coming to get me. I went outside and walked across the street, staring at a couple in front of their house. My vision was a bit blurry, but I could see enough to know that I wanted what they had. They looked peaceful, sober, and fulfilled, standing in front of a nice place. Everyone I saw had something better than me, I was sure of it. I felt defeated. I was headed for jail, again, and I knew heavy withdrawal from drugs and alcohol was on its way. Finally, two police vehicles arrived. After ensuring I was safe and somewhat coherent, the officers placed me in the back of one of the cruisers and took me off to the local county jail, where I'd sit for a day before being trans-ferred to the next county, where the warrant for my arrest had been issued. I sat in the jail cell and began to cry, a drunken cry that would become a regular feature of my life. I sat on the hard concrete floor, cold and shivering, begging for something

THE BEGINNING OF THE END

different, until at last I faded out of consciousness.

At the Steele County Court-house a couple of days later, I met with my public defender. She looked me square in the eye and said, "I don't know who you think you are, or what you think you're dealing with, but this isn't a slap-on-the-wrist kind of trouble. You were set

Name:   LENNOX, JASON ANTHONY

to be put on probation and avoid jail time for this charge, but they're going to recommend a thirty-day sentence now, because you can't show up when you're supposed to." She continued, "I'm telling you this—you need to show up for the scheduled intake day, or you'll be sitting a lot longer than thirty days." In the courtroom, the judge ordered a thirty-day sentence that he'd allow me to start a couple weeks later, to accommodate my request to get my life and job in order first. Of course, I had no job, and it was arguable whether I had a life. I simply wanted to delay that painful experience in jail for as long as I could.

On the Monday morning in March when I was due to show up at the detention center, I sat awake at 1 a.m. After a week-end of hard drinking, I had stayed up all night drinking beer after beer to prepare myself for a couple weeks without any chemicals, trying to drown out my feelings of fear. My room-mate Dan drove me to jail later that morning. Dan was younger than me, just eighteen years old, but was one of the few friends in my group who held a regular job. He was tall and skinny, a stereotypical "geek," with glasses and long, hippie-style hair that was already balding on top. He was a good friend to have living with me, because he fulfilled many needs I couldn't fulfill on my own. He never questioned my drinking or drugging—I think he felt cool hanging out with our crew, and just wanted to be part of the group. As we slowly approached the detention center in Owatonna, I sprayed dozens of shots of Binaca, the strongest of peppermint breath sprays, into my alcohol-saturated mouth. I was confident I'd covered the smell, and I walked into the front office with my head high. I hated that I was about to be locked up, but the beers had taken the edge off, and I knew I had to present as normal and sober.

After some paperwork in the front lobby, I stood and approached the large gray metal door. A loud buzz echoed through the lobby, indicating that the central control center had released the lock. The corrections officer who met me at the door was a large black man with long locks reaching halfway down his back and a slow, smooth walk. I kept my distance as much as possible, walking a step or two behind him so he wouldn't be able to smell any whiff of alcohol. The first hall we walked down had nothing on the brick walls, only lights above and cameras in the corners. Every door and hallway within those walls was locked and required coordinated entry from the control station. It felt like the path was leading me to a dungeon.

We made it to the intake pod, a place I'd seen several times before. There were intake cells all around the sides of the room, with a sitting area between them. Directly ahead, in the center of the space, was a circular desk that faced out on all sides of the unit. To the right were the storage and shower rooms. The officer asked me to change and drop all my belongings into a bucket. Following his command, I put on white boxers and an undershirt, both of which smelled as musty as my grandma's basement, and the orange jumpsuit. As we sat down to complete my paperwork, the officer said, "I'm sure this will come as a huge surprise to you, but you have a strong smell of alcohol coming from you. We're going to need to do a Breathalyzer."

My heart sank. I knew a Breathalyzer meant I'd be in the intake unit for a day or two, and the intake unit was terrible. But policy required inmates to be alcohol-free before entering the general population pods. More importantly, I thought about my probation officer. I had failed to meet her the week before—I had called in stating I was sick, but the truth was that I had been drunk, as I always was when it mattered most. I was terrified the intake officer would call her directly and they would add to my time in jail. When I asked the officer about it, though, he responded carelessly that it wasn't his job to communicate with probation. A small but instant relief.

I spent the next couple weeks counting down my time in the detention center, anxiously awaiting the chance to get back to freedom. While I was there, I made a commitment to myself: I would never go back to using drugs or alcohol. I was tired of the life I lived. I didn't have a job or a home that was legitimately mine, I had lost my friends, I had no relationship with my son, and I had wasted so much potential. I reflected on the high school kid who'd had the brightest of futures. I had been smart, good at sports, and had the ability to do anything I wanted in life. Now, with a couple weeks of sobriety under my belt, I had thoughts for the first time in a long while of becoming all those things again. Free from the chemicals that had forced me into a living hell, I could be a good and active father, a college graduate, a business owner, a productive member of society. My release date arrived, and I was excited to get out and start fresh. I walked into the crisp spring air with a new-found sense of hope, with my head held high, determined to make it this time. As I turned left, toward town, I felt different. I knew this was the time.

# " FIRST YOU TAKE A DRINK, THEN THE DRINK TAKES A DRINK, THEN THE DRINK TAKES YOU.

UNKNOWN

# CHAPTER 8

# POWERLESS

I knocked firmly on the glass door, cupping my eyes to see if anyone inside was coming my way. An employee approached the door and opened it slightly to ask, "Can I help you?" "The sign says you open at 9 a.m. It's 9:02!" I exclaimed, as if he didn't know the time. "I'm sorry," he said, "I got here late and need just a couple more minutes to get opened." I stood there impatiently, waiting for his return. The moment he unlocked the doors, I walked in and went straight for the cheapest bottle of vodka I could find. I snuck around the back of the building across the parking lot, opened the bottle, and took a few swigs. The alcohol burned more than ever, and I had nothing to wash the taste or burn away. At last, my brain returned to a familiar state—relaxed, warm, and able to focus on my day's next moves. I pulled out my phone, turned it on, and called for a ride. I had been out of jail for just an hour and a half.

As I waited for my ride, it occurred to me I had already broken the commitment I had just made to myself. My willpower had given way to the insanity of addiction, again. How had I so quickly forgotten the thoughts and feelings I'd had walking out of that detention center? What had happened to my desire to stay sober and live a new kind of life? Everything else I had ever set out to do—sports, academics, making friends—I could do, and do well. But giving up alcohol and drugs was different. It was as if I couldn't even try some days. And that feeling started the vicious cycle all over again. I wanted something different, failed, then dealt with that failure by doing more of the thing I didn't want to. I had created a significant gap between who I was and who I knew I could and should be, a gap that was filled with pain and suffering. And that pain could only be relieved by drugs and alcohol. In my position, with no job, no home, no car, and no resources, the only way to feed my addiction was to do more things that caused me to drift further from the person I wanted to be. I hurt people, I stole, I lied, I cheated. Whatever it took to fulfill the unconscious and unending desire for an altered state of mind. In those brief moments when I fully realized the gap and felt the pain that came with it, it was almost as if lightning had struck me—I was shocked, paralyzed, and unable to breathe. In fact, I think a lightning strike would have been easier, because at least it would have had an explanation. My drug and alcohol use didn't. I started to accept that it might never be explained, which meant it would never be solved.

I was hanging with my cousin Scott not too long after my release when he posed the most deafening question I can ever remember being asked. After a night of partying, we were smoking cigarettes on his back porch and discussing how much drinking had happened the night before. Scott liked his drinks, for sure, but he also watched the way I drank. I had already had a drink that morning, and it was not even 10 a.m. He looked me in the eyes, piercing to my soul, and asked, "Why do you drink the way you do? And with your family history, your dad's death, and all the trouble you've gotten into, why do you drink at all?" No one had ever asked me in that way—or perhaps, I should say, I had never heard the question quite that way. People had been asking me all my life why I did the things I did, but when he asked, it was different. I don't remember what I said, but I do remember what happened inside my head. As I sat in silence, only three words came to my mind: *I don't know.* For the first time in my life, it occurred to me that I had no excuse, no justification, no sound reason for all my drinking and drugging. In that moment, I began to experience what I later learned was true powerlessness—the inability to stop my addiction, and more importantly, the lack of any reasoning to make it make sense. I was crushed with defeat, sinking in my chair with no hope. If my justifications and reasons for using chemicals weren't there, and I still wasn't stopping, I thought, that meant my life was out of my hands. At that time, it felt like the worst spot I could have ever been in. But in terms of recovery, it was quite possibly the best spot I, or anyone struggling with addiction, could ever be in, because it meant I stopped fighting that I'd be able to change. Letting go of the idea that I had the power inside to stop the addiction was the most important first step toward recovery, but I didn't know it at the time. All I knew then was that any chance at a successful

life was all but over for me. I lived the next couple years dominated by one goal—to minimize the pain and maximize the fun
of the short life I had left. I was sure I'd join my father in suc-
cumbing to this disease at an early age. The only question was:
How long would I last?

...

I worked to bring the building in front of me into focus—half a
block long, two stories high, with windows spanning the length
of each story. I stared at the first-floor hair salon that sat directly
below my apartment. The streetlights lit up the front side of the
building. It was a quiet weeknight with no one in sight. I had
been drinking most of the day, mixing some drugs in earlier on.
I turned the ignition and held it there until the car turned over.
It was my neighbor Allen's car, one he let me borrow often, and
it started slowly every time. After about seven rounds of hearing that ignition try to fire, it finally caught. The red Oldsmobile
smelled terrible, with garbage everywhere and dirt covering the
seats. It worked, though, and that night, that was all I needed. I
reversed out of the parking space and headed out of town.

Out on the main highway, I pushed the pedal down until
I couldn't anymore. My heart began to race, and my thoughts
followed. I watched the speedometer as it passed forty, then
fifty, then sixty. My hands were clammy and shaking as I
gripped the steering wheel and the tears started to well up. The
speedometer passed seventy, then trickled past eighty. I didn't
know how fast the car could go, but I was going to find out. My

breathing was growing intermittent, and I noticed the silence in the car whenever my heavy breathing would pause. As the car reached ninety, the steering wheel began to shake violently. Tears were dripping from my cheeks and the road in front of me was getting blurrier by the second. In the distance was a curve in the road. I thought back to all the hopes and dreams I had had as a kid, as a high schooler, as a suffering adult in a jail cell. I couldn't bear the pain that plagued my every day anymore. I had my chance, rapidly approaching about a mile ahead. With tears streaming, my arms shaking, and my head and heart beyond repair, I cried out, "If you're really out there, God, give me the strength to crank this wheel, just one time." And then, at the top of my lungs, "I can't do this anymore!"

I woke up to light beaming through the window. I opened my eyes and looked around. I saw the familiar, empty walls of my bedroom. How had I gotten there? I touched my arms, looking for a sensation to confirm that I was awake, alive, and unharmed. It didn't make sense—I remembered vividly driving as fast as I could down the highway, then a flash, and all memory was gone. The fact that I was alive brought a mix of emotions. I had often wished I wasn't alive, but it wasn't every day that I came so close to ending my suffering. Usually, fear took over, but the night before had been different. I had taken a trip to the edge of a cliff and stood as if with one foot on the ground and the other reaching out for the drop-off. It took courage to get to that point. I couldn't remember feeling any fear or trying to talk myself out of it, and I had no idea how it had ended with me back home. I looked out the window for the red car—there it sat, as usual.

...

It was a hot summer day, not even noon, and I was drunk. I had been up for days partying and could barely walk straight. My brother Dale and his friend Drew showed up and Dale pulled me aside, telling me he needed a favor.

"Bro, we're going to pick up some pills from someone we don't really know that well. Will you please come with? We'll give you a few, for sure," he assured me. He knew there were two ways to motivate me: feed my ego, and feed my addiction.

We jumped into Drew's old beater truck and smoked cigarette after cigarette on our way down the back country roads. We were on a familiar route, curving around corners we often took to family gatherings at my uncle's or my grandpa's. The windows were down, air moving through the cab, and classic rock booming from the radio. My brother told me we were meeting out in the country to avoid seeing any police. We took a last turn down the gravel road that led to my grandpa's farm. Driving past the white fence that surrounded the pasture, I thought back to all the summers I had to paint that dang fence. As we approached the main house, my brother exclaimed, "Look, Mom is here, and so is Uncle Jesse and Uncle Shane! Should we stop?"

"Yes!"

I was drunk, high, and carefree, ready to socialize. The huge white farmhouse had a concrete porch that spanned the entire length of the house. I led the way up the three concrete stairs and quickly opened the screen door. On the other side, I was shocked to find the dining table full of people. My grandma, my mom, my uncle, a probation officer; Liz, a county assessor I had met a few times before; and another face I didn't recognize, a petite old man with wrinkled skin, long gray hair, and a bald patch across the top of his head. Looking at their faces, I quickly realized something was wrong. The older man introduced himself: "I'm Jack, and I'm an interventionist."

Suddenly, I understood. Scared, upset, and completely caught off guard, I turned to do what I did best—run. Immediately behind me, my brother and Drew stood blocking the door. I stared into my brother's eyes and saw a fear I had never seen in him before, but he stood his ground, shoulder to shoulder with Drew. I turned around again, looking straight through the kitchen doorway, and rushed to get to the back door, but I didn't make it far. My two uncles closed the gap.

"Please, Jason, just listen to us for a minute," my uncle Shane begged. He was also terrified. They knew they were dealing with a different version of Jason, along with an addiction that baffled them as much as it did me. I was irate, and knowing that probation workers were in the room, I cursed everyone for jeopardizing my freedom. I stormed into the living room, dropped down on the love seat, and put my head in my hands. I was sweating, shaking, and so upset with myself for having fallen for this. My next high was clearly not happening, and now I was stuck in a corner, with nowhere to run. One by one, family, friends, and counseling staff took turns trying to talk to me. Jack, the interventionist, was the one that got the closest to a genuine conversation.

"Can't you see me?" I blurted to him. "I'm so upset right now, I can't go to treatment. I can't believe they would do this to me," I muttered, shaking my head aggressively. "Please, Jack, we need to do this another day."

After many failed attempts to negotiate, Jack agreed to meet me the following Thursday in Owatonna. As I did with most of the agreements I made during that period of life, I broke that one with Jack. I never made it to our planned meeting, and I never saw him again.

...

One year into my probation, I was living a rocky life, bouncing between partying and wishing my life was over. One of the requirements of my probation was a quarterly group supervision meeting. Along with hundreds of others, I would show up, wait in line, confirm my contact information, and listen to a lecture by a guest speaker, usually about the negative impacts of a life of confinement. I paid very little attention—all I needed to do was hang on long enough to get out of there and get back to partying. At first, I had figured out how to play it safe for those meetings: I would stop doing drugs and drinking a couple days before the meeting, knowing most of what I had consumed would be out of my system within seventy-two hours. But after the first few meetings, I realized they were a breeze and the risk was low. So when my buddy Dan drove me into my next meeting one winter morning, I hadn't even bothered stopping in time for the meeting.

Dan parked the car outside the large armory building and prepared to do what he usually did—take a nap for what he

anticipated would be an hour or so. When I walked in, I immediately noticed something markedly different. At the front
of the room were buckets. I couldn't tell what was in them,
but my heart sank and my stomach turned as I realized that
some of us were being asked to provide urine samples. How
could this happen? I thought I had figured the system out! As I
neared the front of the line, I noticed that on the packets being
handed out, a line was highlighted for some, and not for others. That one line held my fate. I prayed to God, begging him to
let me slide this time, promising him this was a wake-up call
that would change me. I was next in line, waiting with sweaty
hands, a pale face, and a tense stance.

"Name, please."

"Jason Lennox," I muttered. As I stood waiting, tense and
pale with sweaty hands, he grabbed the middle pile, pulled back
a few other packets, and handed me mine. Like a brick wall
collapsing on itself, my hope for escape dropped in an instant.
With a single line of highlighter, my nightmare had begun—I
was one of the unlucky few selected to provide a sample. He
directed me to another man near the entrance door. I had no
idea what I was going to do, but I knew I couldn't go back to
jail. As we approached the men's bathroom, I told the officer
I needed to let my ride know it was going to be a bit longer.
Instead, as soon as I got outside I jumped into Dan's car, star-
tling him from his nap, and told him we had to leave.

"What's going on?" he asked, confused.

"Just get out of here!" I shouted urgently. Frantic as we
drove down the highway, I explained the situation to him. The
only way I could see out of this was to go to the hospital with

an emergency. The problem was, the only emergency happening was in my head. There was nothing wrong with me besides my thought process.

How had I gotten here? All I had to do was stay sober for three days before a meeting. There were only four meetings a year, and I knew a year in advance when they were. Four times. Three days. A total of just twelve days of sobriety a year, and I couldn't do it. Instead, three days before the meeting, I convinced myself that if I just drank more water the next day, I could party for one more night. When two days remained, I thought, I could always just take a pill that would flush my system. And when one day remained—well, what the hell was the point by then? I'd roll the dice and hope for the best. But the dice had gone the other way.

After some sound advice from Dan, a moment of clarity returned me to the armory building. When the officer asked where I had gone, I told him I wasn't feeling well. I walked into the bathroom, kicked the second stall open and dropped to my knees, grasping the toilet seat and making gagging sounds as best I could. I thought I was good at acting, but the officer stood behind me, watched the show I was putting on, and then asked me to stand up.

"I'm not stupid, man," he said. "Tell me what's going on, and do us both a favor and be honest." I bowed my head in silence, all my strength gone.

"What do you want from me?" I cried.

"Here's the deal—you can skip all the BS and save us a drug test, time, and money, and sign this piece of paper stating you've used drugs or alcohol. We'll work with you."

I was worried about going back to jail, but he assured me that if I did the right thing, they wouldn't take me that day. He explained I'd need an assessment to determine whether treatment was where I belonged. I took him up on the offer, signed the form, and promised to go to the assessment clinic immediately. As I walked out of that building, I felt a sense of relief and gratitude at having escaped another trip to the most painful place I knew, the six-by-nine-foot jail cell. I breathed in the fresh winter air and thanked the universe for the second chance. Back in Dan's car, I explained the entire incident with a sincerity and authenticity that was rare for me. I was ready this time. I knew my chances of staying out of jail completely were slim, but the officer had guaranteed me that *without* the assessment, jail was in my near future. A mile and a half down the road, we pulled up to the long, single-story building that housed the county's chemical health department. I walked through the doors with my head down.

"How can I help you?" the kind woman behind the desk asked.

"I need a chemical health assessment," I muttered.

"It looks like we have an opening later this week, Thursday morning," she said. I agreed to it and took an appointment card. As I walked out of that building, I prepared myself to be completely real with someone about my drug and alcohol use for the first time. My partial admission to the man earlier that morning had brought a surprising relief, and I wanted more of that. I'd be back in three days, three days I could bring to the table sober. Sober sounded good. And I knew it was my only way out.

...

I never went back for the assessment I scheduled. I never made it to court for the probation violation related to my drug use. With felony warrants out for my arrest, my life had become one big ball of fear. I awoke on a warm, spring day, hardly able to sit up. I had a pounding headache and felt like I was going to vomit. The weight of the most terror I'd ever experienced was suffocating me. I reached for my phone and frantically scrolled through for anyone who might have something that could help—street drugs, prescription pills, alcohol, anything to lift this fear. My search, as usual, ended without much luck. If I was going to find anything, I knew I'd need to go out and face the world, something I hated doing. I put a pair of shoes on, searched the apartment for cigarette butts that might still have a puff or two left, and headed for the stairs. As I opened the door at the bottom of the stairs, the sun overwhelmed me. I turned right and headed for the apartment of a new friend I had just met. Cars were coming from both directions, and as I crossed the busy street, fear crippled me again. I put my head down and stormed forward hoping no one in any of the cars would see or know me. I had hurt so many people in that small town, whether they knew it or not, and every time the dust settled and the chemicals wore off, I was left with the feelings of guilt, shame, and remorse that dominated my life. Being outside was like being naked, exposing myself to all those I had harmed and to the law enforcement officers I knew would eventually find me.

As I traversed the next block, my sense of terror heightened. The sound of a house door closing startled me and I sped up, hyperventilating. My body shook with fear, as if I were running from a horror story's murderer. As I rounded the corner and spotted the door to John's apartment building, I felt a moment of relief. But I knew all the buildup might be for nothing; I didn't even know if he was home. At this point I had burned bridges with most of the people in my life, so keeping my addiction fed depended on the newer friendships I had made. I walked through the outside doors and knocked on the door of John's unit. I heard a child's voice coming from the inside, a good sign. John and his wife invited me in. It was still morning, and I didn't know what day it was, but John was always willing to drink a few beers with me—it was a big part of the reason we connected. After a couple more, I asked if I could borrow eight dollars to cover the cost of a bottle of vodka. To my surprise, instead he offered me a bottle of his vodka, which was a step up from the cheapest bottle I usually bought. I took it gratefully and headed for the comfort of my second-floor apartment, away from everyone else, where I drank myself into oblivion.

The binge that followed wiped out most of my conscious memory of the next week, and I woke up several days later in the worst shape of my life. I was still drunk enough that the pounding headache and sickness hadn't fully kicked in yet, but I struggled to stand, go to the bathroom, or even sit up straight without feeling like I was going to collapse. I got a glass of water and sat down in my large blue recliner by the long windows that lined the front of the building. The coffee table was littered with empty packs of cigarettes, a couple beer cans, and a dirty dish from some sort of concoction I must have put together in the preceding days. I hurt as much as I ever had.

My body craved water, but as I reached out my left hand to grab the large tumbler I'd poured, something felt terribly wrong. I couldn't squeeze my hand. My hand trembled and didn't have the strength to close around the cup. Using both hands, I managed to press the cup between my palms and slowly lift it to my mouth. As soon as I managed to swallow a few sips, I immediately felt the water wanting to come back up. I slowly made my way to the bathroom and crawled to the toilet, where I threw up the little bit of water I had drunk. The water tasted of poison— sour and bitter, like the taste of a pill sitting a moment too long on the tongue before being swallowed. The dry heaving that followed showed there was nothing else in my body to come up. Somehow I managed to make it back to my chair. Even if I had been able to get the water glass to my mouth, I couldn't drink; nothing would stay down. My motor functions were failing, my internal organs were rejecting any liquid or solid, and my body was a shell of what it once was. I curled up under a blanket and prayed for sleep.

A couple hours later, I opened my eyes again to a pain even more intense than before. It felt like a pair of pliers was squeezing each eye. I knew I needed to get out of that building. I messaged my cousin Scott, asking if I could come stay with him for a weekend, and he agreed to pick me up the next day. Throughout the rest of that day and night I suffered through increasing sickness, though I was slowly regaining my motor functions. The next day, Scott came by and scooped me up. I played shortstop on Scott's softball team—that is, if and when I managed to go to the games—and when he picked me up, we headed right to the softball practice he had scheduled. It didn't take me long to realize I needed to stay out of the infield. I had no reaction time and put myself in a bad spot standing in front of some of those balls. Even if I did stop a ball, I couldn't coordinate my extremities enough to throw it to first base. I was scared everyone would notice. The last couple days were becoming clear, and I realized I had had such a long and hard binge that my body had shut down. I could only hope there would be no lasting effects.

Recovering from the binge had a silver lining, though—I didn't have much time to think about the relationship I had just lost. A few days earlier, enraged and in a drunken stupor, I had made a scene and threatened to leave the state. It was something I did regularly to get attention, but this time, I had crossed the line for the last time, and my girlfriend Ashley had had enough. As I regained my physical abilities, I thought more about my life situation. I was twenty-three years old, living off others, with no job and no resources. I was facing a wall of trouble, including felony warrants, probation violations, check fraud, and many other legal troubles. The wall leaned more by the day, and I knew it would crash down on me eventually. I just hoped I would be dead by the time it happened.

In recovering from my latest destructive binge, I finally found the courage, strength, and willingness to give up drinking and drugging—well, mostly. In the early days of recouping, I turned to marijuana again. It calmed my anxiety, but more importantly, it created some consistency in my life. I stopped partying all night, drinking massive amounts of liquor, and searching for stimulants and pills, and I began to get regular nutrition. To put it simply, I was replenishing my body with all it had been missing: rest, food, and water. I spent more time with my cousin and our family, and I started to feel a little life in me again. The feeling that came from seeing police officers and the fear of facing my felony troubles always lingered, but I found that enough pot could usually help me forget that reality.

> For what felt like the first time in my life, I began to think about how to repair some of the damage I had done to the people around me.

For what felt like the first time in my life, I began to think about how to repair some of the damage I had done to the people around me. I was like a tornado that had come crashing into the lives of those close to me, quickly damaging everything in proximity, then just as quickly disappearing. I got in touch with a few buddies who had been hardest hit, offered my apologies, and asked what I could do to restore the relationships—or at least to restore those friends to where they were before my tornado had ripped through their lives. Even when I received no response, or a bad response, there was something incredibly freeing about the experience. I hadn't necessarily found a way to repair all my broken relationships or to face my legal troubles, but at least I had stopped doing damage. That was a big win, relatively speaking. And it gave me a glimmer of hope I hadn't felt for a long time. I had some fun that summer and started to remember how to smile and laugh. I watched others drink, and there wasn't much in me that wanted to go back to it. I was rocked by the memory of my failing motor functions, and I knew staying away from alcohol was a condition of living with my cousin. We had a lot of fun playing softball and yard games and working late at night refinishing floors. I felt purpose again. Though emotionally I still felt weighed down by my impending legal problems, I was going to enjoy my physical freedom for as long as I could.

"

# HITTING BOTTOM AND HITTING IT HARD WAS THE WORST THING THAT EVER HAPPENED TO ME AND THE BEST THING THAT EVER HAPPENED TO ME.

DAVE RAMSEY

# CHAPTER 9

# THE FINAL FALL

I walked into a job orientation one Monday morning and immediately succumbed to an overwhelming sense of fear—there, just ahead with his back to me, was a tall, uniformed sheriff. My body tensed up and I proceeded to sit as far in the back as I could. I had landed a job with a group home, but I wasn't aware until that moment that the orientation would include some training from law enforcement. I kept my head down, buried deep in the materials in my orientation folder, and did everything I could to avoid eye contact with the officer. The sheriff had a small underbite, wavy dark brown hair, and a neatly trimmed goatee. He stood in the front of the room and shared a ton of information, but I didn't hear a word of it—I was laser-focused on the fact that this man could be the difference between a free Jason and a locked-up Jason. After what seemed like hours, the few minutes of his presentation had passed and the officer went on his way.

I was training to become a caretaker for developmentally disabled adults. Although as a young child I'd had plenty of experiences caring for others, I had never imagined finding a job like that. I realized quickly that caring for others created a feeling of value like none I had ever experienced—I was *needed* when I was there. That felt good, and of course doing the responsible work thing felt good, too. I landed the overnight sleep shift, which worked doubly well for me—I got paid to sleep, and I had a place to sleep. I had abandoned my apartment, which I hadn't really been paying for, so I slept on the couch of the group home where I worked four to five nights a week. Whenever I could, I picked up shifts before and after, which was also convenient, as I didn't have many places I could go. Though I didn't have a lot of resources, I was making a living wage, keeping myself from doing more damage, and contributing to the lives of those who needed it most.

One Friday afternoon in late October, I finally had a weekend off. I had been working a ton of hours and I knew I had some money coming my way. I smoked a bowl of pot with my buddy Joe, then had a nap at his place while he took off for a friend's. When I woke up, I messaged Joe and he told me he was hanging in his friend's garage on the other side of town. He said he'd be back in a bit and urged me to stay put, because he knew I had been off the "other" drugs and drinking and didn't want to put me in that position. After we hung up, I sat in Joe's living room, watching the sun start to set, and I felt a sense of depression set in. The mere thought of using meth again had the power to quickly change my perception, making my life suddenly feel bleak and boring. I had been smoking pot but free of other drugs and alcohol for four months now, and it was getting old. *Screw it*, I thought. *I'll be okay with a night of fun.* I messaged Joe back and told him I was fine, that a night of partying wouldn't hurt me. He called again to try to deter me, but I rationalized that I had a job, I had paychecks coming, and I had already learned my lesson the hard way. High on drugs himself, Joe was easy to convince and agreed to pick me up. I went outside to wait anxiously on the sidewalk for him. It was a different kind of anxious, though—I felt like I was under-water, swimming toward the surface, knowing at the peak of the climb was a breath of air. The cravings took over, my mind raced, and I couldn't wait to experience the feeling I could so vividly recall.

When we arrived back at his friend's house, Joe pulled up the gravel driveway and we walked into the open, high-ceilinged garage, which had a concrete floor and a lounge area near the back. Joe's buddy Dusty stood up to introduce himself with a smile and a handshake, and I thanked him for letting me stop by. Every feeling I had was intensified as I got closer to that euphoria. Dusty was warm, his place was welcoming, and the colors were vibrant. I admired the bright red of the couch, and I thought each of the disorganized supplies on the table looked to be in exactly the right place. I was shaking as I awaited the next round of hits on the meth pipe. They each took a turn with the pipe, then passed it my way. Hardly able to breathe, I exhaled, put the pipe to my lips, and began burning the crystal substance in the pipe. I spun that pipe and watched the smoke explode inside, slowly taking it in for as long as I could, then all at once I released the pipe and inhaled as fast and hard as possible. My skin and face tingled as I let out a cloud of smoke so dense, I couldn't see through it, and my body immediately dropped a couple inches. Finally, relief had returned. I knew then that it was all going to be okay again. I was back.

After a night of partying hard, Joe and I headed for his parents' place; they were away for the weekend. I wanted to find some more drugs and keep the party going, but Joe was ready for a nap. He told me not to mess with anything in the house and headed upstairs, saying, "Crash on the couch, if you want," as he walked around the corner. A familiar feeling hit me. I was the last one awake, the only one still wondering how I was going to get my next fix. I had long ago realized there was something different about my drug and alcohol use. Even the drug dealers and heaviest drug users I hung out with sometimes thought it was a good idea to stop. I was often urged to get a little rest and start again with a refreshed mind and body, but that never made sense to me. I couldn't understand any reason for stopping the party—I would only stop if I ran out, passed out, or was locked up. When the "worst of the worst" were crashing while I searched for more, I knew something was wrong. It wasn't just the rest of the world that looked at me like I was a wasted example of life, that laughed at me and wished me away. Even the heaviest partyers wondered what was wrong with me.

There in Joe's parents' living room, I had barely thought about rest before I turned back to my phone, searching for any name I associated with more drugs. I had to be careful, because so many people in my life knew I was making strides. I spent hours reaching out to anyone I could think of, getting a little more desperate by the minute. On that day, my search ended without any luck, and I left Joe's place later that afternoon while he was still asleep. But of course, that one time using meth led to another, and another led to another. Before I knew it, I was off to the races, drinking and using as problematically as ever. As those around me began to question my sobriety again, I slowly distanced myself from everyone. I was riddled with denial, shame, guilt, and remorse most days, and all the hope I had gained in a four-month span free from hard drugs and alcohol was gone. My tolerance was back to its highest point, the effects of drugs and alcohol on my system were back to their lowest point, and my inevitable destiny was around the corner. I was out of steam, out of fight, and at twenty-four, I felt I had lived enough of a life to call it quits.

...

On December 8, 2010, I woke up with a paycheck I wasn't used to having. I didn't feel the greatest. That's what happened when I didn't have the right combination of drugs and alcohol in my system. By that point in my life, twelve years into my addiction, I could only experience a sense of balance and ease if I aligned the right amount of chemicals with the right environment. I had to work at two o'clock and knew I would need to act fast to fulfill the need inside me. I messaged a connection and asked about getting a bag of methamphetamines. He said he could make it happen, and the relief I felt was instantaneous. A deep and satisfying breath followed. It was going to be okay again. Contrary to what many believe, the addiction is often satisfied long before the physical effects of a drug are felt—the psychological impact can be just as important. Knowing my drugs were on their way, I prepared the rest of what I needed for that day, brushing my teeth and getting my travel bag together. I was sleeping on a friend's couch yet again, this time in an apartment building I had once managed. I needed a kickstart while waiting, so I went to the kitchen and found the container of Folgers. I made a glass, but not in the normal way—instead I just mixed the grounds with cold water and drank the whole thing, chewing on the grounds as I slammed the glass down. It tasted like a mix of sour and bitter, and that's where my life was. Ironically, I don't know if the unbrewed coffee even had its normal caffeinating effect, but nonetheless, on I went.

I met my connection and immediately headed to the most inconspicuous space I could find, the downstairs space of my friend's apartment building, which I had set up for big parties back when I'd managed the building. There was a pool table and a couch, and a lot of empty alcohol cans and bottles. The place smelled like a barroom at 2 a.m. after the doors closed. But it was dark and quiet, and no one would know I was there. I found a glass pipe, dropped some of the meth—the most powerful drug I had in my arsenal—into the center, and began to burn it down. Usually, the feeling that followed a hit off a pipe like that was overwhelmingly satisfying. Exhaling the smoke was exhilarating, like the feeling after an intense workout, or after a bite of the best ice cream on the planet, but multiplied infinitely. Instant joy and happiness. On this day, though, it felt a little different. Maybe it was the batch, I thought, or maybe it was my state of mind. I smoked some more and went back upstairs, wondering how I could enhance my feelings. But first, I needed a ride to work.

My brother John agreed to come get me and drive me the fifteen miles back to his own town, where I worked. Along the way, I asked him to stop at a liquor store. It was only about noon, so I knew I had to have some excuse.

"My coworkers aren't twenty-one and they want some alcohol for tonight," I said. "I'll be working when the stores close, so I need to grab it now."

The walk through the liquor store always created a feeling of guilt and shame in me. Most people in my life assumed I didn't drink anymore—or at least, that's what I thought. In reality, most of them certainly knew better. But in the state I was in, thinking I was fooling everyone, buying liquor always felt like it exposed the truth. I bought the cheapest one-liter bottle of vodka they had, and we headed to my cousin's place.

My cousin Scott had a nice house on the corner of one of the busier streets in town. Cars flew by all day long. The house had two levels, a basketball hoop outside, and the nicest carpet I'd ever seen inside the entry door in the clean, organized garage. After saying hi, I asked to use the shower. Certainly, I could have used one, as I'd been wearing the same clothes for several days, the couch I slept on was far from clean, and I smelled like a boys' locker room: sweaty, musty, and quite ripe. But the real reason I wanted to shower was to get some drinks in from that bottle of vodka. In the bathroom, I turned the fan on to drown out the sound as I twisted the vodka bottle open. I knew it would taste terrible, but I also knew I needed it. I thought I might have taken too much of the drugs and whenever that happened, alcohol could bring me back down. I poured a glass of water from the bathroom sink, knowing I couldn't drink the vodka without something behind it. It was warm, cheap, and as disgusting as any alcohol product I'd ever had. It felt like I was drinking something poisonous, and frankly, that's what it was. But the minute the bottle hit my lips, I felt an instant relief, accompanied by the feeling that I was going to throw up. The liquid burned my mouth, filled my nose, and forced its way past the repulsion of my throat. Immediately, without breathing, I slammed a glass of water. It dulled the sickening taste only slightly, but more importantly, it pushed the vodka down my esophagus. One drink down and several to go. I fought through the nausea and headache it caused, and each drink got just a bit easier. Finally, I could relax for a minute. I heard my cousin in the living room and wondered if he thought about what I was doing. He knew I wasn't well. Everyone knew.

I stood in the shower and let the hot, steamy water hit my body, enjoying one of the few things other than drugs that offered a brief sensation of physical satisfaction. I still didn't feel the best and couldn't tell why. The meth and alcohol should have had me on cloud nine, feeling all sorts of joy and excitement. But not that day. I thought perhaps the wear and tear of running from the police for nearly a year, knowing it was all going to come crashing down at some point, was taking a long-term toll that couldn't be drowned out so easily anymore. I was tired, I was sick, and most of all, I was hopeless. I just wanted some peace in my life, but I knew that peace would never be part of my story. Not if I kept running, and not while I continued to go deeper into addiction. But I had to keep trying, I had to kick that feeling.

I finished my shower, dressed quickly, and packed my bag again, hiding the bottle under my clothes. My brother gave me a ride to the group home across town, where I took care of four elderly adults, all disabled in some way. Though I had only had the job for two months, it had given me a sense of meaning and a feeling of usefulness. In every other aspect of my life, I knew I was a burden on those around me, and especially on society. At the group home, though, I was needed. What a feeling.

On this day, however, sickness was taking over. Not only was I not feeling the greatest, I was also very disappointed that the drugs and alcohol were not working as usual. I had very limited resources, many times none at all, so to use them up and still be suffering was dreadful. My brother dropped me off and as I watched him pull away in his truck, I wished I had the freedom that I imagined he did, a freedom that I was so far from. I walked in to meet the on-duty staff member, assuming as always that I could play off the effects and smells of the drugs and alcohol. I doubt she bought it as she shared her report of the day and we exchanged control of the environment.

It was a normal Wednesday at the house for everyone but me. Left alone with the guys, I knew I needed to feel better. As soon as I'd checked in with each of them, I headed down the old, cracked, wooden stairs to the basement. Waiting for me at the bottom was a cold concrete floor, and there was a musty, moist smell in the air. I flipped the light on and found the washer and dryer. I'd decided to try the drugs first and see how that worked, and I needed a surface to crush them on. I finished what I had and felt some relief, but not enough. I took a few shots of liquor and headed back upstairs to hang with the guys. I took a seat on the couch. One of the guys sat in his wheelchair next to me, while another came down and rocked back and forth on his feet, telling me all about his day. I couldn't hear much of it, though. I stared off into the sun that shone in through the window behind him.

I remember thinking there had to be something better. I knew I was nearing the end of a road that would have me crashing into reality. The end of my life seemed like a better destination. I knew I needed to tend to the house and my job, but I just couldn't get motivated or shake the negative feeling I had. I had done all the drugs I had and had drunk a bunch of vodka with no relief. Where else could I turn? I messaged a cousin for some prescription pain pills and arranged for him to come to the house. Those would definitely take the edge off, I thought, and bring me back to life.

Within an hour, I had my next vice in hand. I popped a few pills and waited. Again, I felt the instant psychological relief of knowing a better feeling was on the way. But it didn't come. I popped the rest of the pills—five more. Even in my altered state I wasn't sure it was the best idea, but I couldn't think of any other way to numb the pain. After another half hour, though I felt a little relief, I also knew something wasn't right. But I wasn't worried—I had been there before, certainly I would level off.

114

A couple hours later, my coworker returned with the groceries. After she finished unloading them, she went into the office to reconcile the money and receipts. I knew I needed to keep my distance. Between the smell of vodka and the shape I was in, I couldn't let her get close. From the office she called, "Is everything okay, Jason?"

"Yeah, I just don't feel the best today, but I'll be okay."

She went on her way, leaving me alone to care for the guys, and that's when I knew. It was over. Something in me just knew that my journey was ending.

As I began to move in and out of different states of consciousness, I can recall picking up the phone and dialing emergency services. I don't know exactly what I said, but I admitted I had gone overboard and that I was fading from consciousness. I can remember a feeling of relief in that moment that I hadn't felt in a long time. Maybe I thought it was all over and my life would really end at that house, or maybe my intuition knew something else was in store for me. Either way, the fighting and the running were over.

"

# EVEN IN THE MIDST OF DEVASTATION, SOMETHING WITHIN US ALWAYS POINTS THE WAY TO FREEDOM.

SHARON SALZBERG

# CHAPTER 10

# LAST CHANCE

When I awoke in the hospital after my nearly fatal final day of use, my eyes opened like an old garage door stuck on the tracks, heavy and hard to move. I had to squint to see. I looked to my left, and the sun turned the room into a fluorescent white space. Through the light, I spotted my coworker Cori. Wells of tears filled her eyes as she cried out, "Jason, you might have lost your job, but at least you didn't lose your life!" Strangely enough, in that moment, all I could focus on was that "might"—I heard that I *might* have lost my job, which meant I *might not* have. The job that I had held for two months, longer than any other job I'd had for years, was more important to me than my near loss of life.

As I lay in the hospital bed, helpless and hopeless, medicated, sedated, and closely monitored after having my stomach pumped, there wasn't much to me. A few immediate family members came to visit when they found out what had happened. My younger brother Dale, who was the closest of all my family members, later recalled to me how he stood at the end of my bed watching my slow and labored breathing. For most of my life, he had looked up to me, and in that moment, he was forced to look down on my all-but-lifeless body. As I came to consciousness for a moment, my eyes opened slightly, and two simple words came out: "I'm sorry."

I *was* sorry. I was sorry for my actions. I was sorry for who I was. I was sorry for all the pain and suffering I had caused others. Most of all, I was sorry for having wasted a precious life. I couldn't understand why I had lived through that day.

The next two days were the worst of my life. I was transferred from that hospital to the intake cell at the detention center, where I'd be left alone with my thoughts and feelings. I thought about all the people who must have heard what had happened. I was a fake, and now everyone knew. And after being on the run for almost a year, my freedom was lost. I sat in my cell, cold and shivering, praying for a way out I knew wouldn't come. I was trapped, literally and figuratively. All the possibilities of escape crossed my mind. Bail? There was none. Medication or treatment for withdrawal? The jail didn't care. That left death. I wondered if I could wrap the thin sheet around something strong enough to hold my body weight. The silence was loud, and the emptiness was full. I couldn't see anything through any lens but regret. I thought of all the chances I'd had to build a new life, all the instances of renewed hope that I had thrown away.

Down forty pounds in the past year, I curled up what was left of my body under the sheet, crippled and crying, bouncing in and out of foggy moments. At times, I believed it was all a nightmare and that I'd wake up soon. Other moments had me begging God to turn back time so I could do things differently. I would have given anything for the chance to go back and change the course of so many moments—anything. But when the fog cleared, reality always

## After being on the run for almost a year, my freedom was lost.

returned. I might not have died, but my life felt like it was over.

And then, through all the other thoughts about how to escape, a new thought came—the intervention! I had to call those people who had been part of my family's intervention a year and a half earlier. I wasn't ready yet to talk to them about seeking the "better life" they insisted I could have, but I was ready to feel anything other than the suffocation of that cold, silent jail cell. I asked my mom to make a call to Liz, the Waseca County assessor who had examined me multiple times. I had told Liz lie after lie in the past, and now my fate rested in her hands.

The call came over the intercom: "Lennox, you're heading to a conference room." My door buzzed open, echoing inside the concrete walls. I walked through the hallways, escorted by a corrections officer and accompanied by a loud buzz at each door, until we reached what they considered a conference room. It looked and felt like the rest of the jail—a far cry from any place you'd hold a standard meeting. The door opened and I hesitantly walked through the door. Full of shame and guilt, I could only half meet Liz's gaze. She smiled, and out of nowhere, all my emotions and words came crashing out.

"I'm so sorry I lied all these years. I've been so sick, and I hate myself right now."

"I knew better," she replied. "But we're not here to make you feel worse." Instead, she assured me, she was in the mood to get the truth and make a recommendation to the judge, who I was scheduled to see the next day.

For the first time ever, I got honest about my use and how bad it was. One by one, the real stories of my addiction poured out. I wanted to continue that assessment for hours, because it felt as close to freedom as I had ever been. But Liz ended the session after an hour, leaving me with hope for something different: "I'm going to find you a bed in treatment," she said. "I'll send the referral to Fountain Centers in Albert Lea and send the recommendation to the judge." I couldn't believe, after all my lies and deceit, that she was still willing to work on my behalf.

The next day, the judge agreed to Liz's recommendation, with the condition that I return to jail once my treatment was complete. The relief hit me all at once. I didn't know what treatment would be like—in fact, I didn't have much hope that it could solve my problems, since I'd long since accepted there was no help for me—but I was going to be removed from that hell inside the brick walls. Anything had to feel better than jail did.

Back at the detention center, I packed my bedding up and waited impatiently for the call that would start my discharge process. Finally, I was ready to walk through the locked door. The buzz sounded, the door opened, and all that was left between me and the fresh winter air was the lobby. As I walked around the back-to-back rows of lobby chairs, I heard my name.

"Jas."

It was my cousin Jen, who worked in management at the detention center. Jen was of medium height, but stood with a posture that meant business. She gave me a glimpse of her big and beautiful smile, and I turned toward her with my head halfway down. It wasn't the first time she had watched me walk through those doors, and it was incredibly embarrassing to know she had seen me there time and time again. Jen gave me a look that I'll never forget—a mix of hard love and compassion.

"Please, you have to get it right this time," she begged.

Her words silenced everything else. "I will," I replied, and I meant it—I had an honest desire to follow through. But I also had a lot of experience where my honest desire didn't last more than minutes. I was scared. Jen was right. I knew I had to get it right this time. It was my last chance.

...

My mom had agreed to drive me to the treatment center, but first, she drove toward her house in New Richland, where I would grab a few extra pieces of clothing to take with me. On the way, I grabbed my phone from my bag and hit the power button, hoping it would turn on after sitting idle for a week. When it did, I almost automatically reached out to Dusty with the idea that I might score a couple hits of pot before entering treatment. For the entirety of the twenty-five-minute drive, I watched my phone anxiously, plotting ways to meet Dusty, smoke a little, and get back into the car without alerting my mom. I had just heard a judge offer me one last chance at freedom, and I sincerely wanted to stay out of trouble this time, but those feelings were no match for the power of my addiction. All normal fear and logic were so quickly replaced by a subconscious need to get drunk or high. Fortunately for me, the reply from Dusty never came, and we left New Richland and started the twenty-minute journey south to Albert Lea. As we neared our destination, my mom asked if I wanted to stop and see my grandma, who was in a nearby nursing home rehabilitating from a fall. She was also sick with cancer, and it happened to be her birthday that day, December 16. I wanted very badly to stop, but I was terrified of not getting to treatment on time and getting into trouble. So even though moments earlier I'd been ready to throw my chance away for just one hit of pot, I passed on stopping to see Grandma. She wasn't far away, I reasoned, and I could get to see her soon enough.

I walked through the large sliding doors of the Albert Lea hospital. The treatment program was on the lower level, and the security officer at the front desk called downstairs to let them know I had arrived. A staff member walked through the door to greet me with a genuine smile. The poofy volume of her faded blond hair gave her a noticeable presence. She welcomed both me and my mom with a handshake. "I'm Sue," she said. She let my mom know she'd take good care of me, and that we'd have to say goodbye there in the lobby. As my mom hugged me, reassuring me she'd be back soon, I was filled with gratitude she was still around after all the years of trouble I had brought our family. I felt a few tears come on as I watched her walk away. Sue gently placed her hand on my shoulder and told me there would be visiting opportunities three times per week.

Downstairs in my new unit, she asked if I wanted anything to eat before we finished the intake process. I was full, having just eaten Burger King on the way over from jail, but I said yes anyway. I had developed problematic eating behaviors over the years—not knowing where my next meal would come from, I'd take any opportunity I could to eat. When given the chance, I would often overeat so much that I'd end up throwing it all up, then I would eat again, and repeat. And even without the food insecurity, I'd eat almost anything to kickstart my endorphins. I sought pleasure in any way I could, and when drugs and alcohol weren't available, food was usually next on the list. I'm sure if I had ever shared this with anyone, I would have quickly been diagnosed with an eating disorder, but shame and embarrassment crushed me and kept me from telling the truth to anyone.

I chowed down in the cafeteria and sure enough, found myself in the bathroom, too full to keep the food in my stomach. When I made it back from the bathroom, we finished the intake process. Sue explained how treatment worked and talked me through my fears and worries. She was a sweet woman and made me feel like I had someone on my side. I hadn't felt support like that in a long time, so I was careful not to ruin it by oversharing. I was terrified to talk about what my life was really like. I thought that surely anyone who knew my story would immediately shun me.

It had been a long and emotional day, and finally Sue escorted me to my new room. It was all the way at the end of the hall, the last room on the left before the locked doors that led to the patio. I chose the first of two beds, next to the bathroom; for the time being, the other bed was open and I would have the room to myself. After unpacking, I plopped down on my back on the bed and stared at the ceiling. I was overwhelmed and tired. This place was so much better than a jail cell, but that didn't take away all the guilt and shame I was feeling. There were so many people I knew I had to face and make things right with. Sitting with my thoughts, I bounced in and out of sleep that entire night.

I knew I had one opportunity, and I was all in.

Sleep began to come more quickly each night, especially after the staff gave me some lavender to put under my pillow and some chamomile tea to help relax me. Being at the center got easier each day that first week. I had almost nothing to my name, and I knew I faced an uphill climb and a potential future back in jail. But somehow I was excited to get up and live life each day, free of all chemicals. It was a feeling I hadn't had since my early childhood. Some call that the "treatment high" or the "pink cloud," and it's a common temporary feeling associated with getting sober. Looking back on it, I believe that feeling came from honestly trying to live the right life and repair relationships. I had sent out a bunch of Christmas cards explaining where I was and what I was hoping to get out of treatment. I was making a real effort to change for the better, even if I didn't believe it would work. I knew I had one opportunity, and I was all in. I was slowly shifting my thoughts and perspective. Instead of focusing on all the things of the past and all that I had done wrong, I was considering what might be possible in the future and all that I was trying to make right. The needle was moving, finally. But just a week into treatment, I was hit with one of the hardest blows I would ever experience, in or out of addiction.

. . .

"Jason, you have visitors," the treatment tech informed me.

Instantly, alarm bells went off in my head. I didn't have any visitors scheduled that day. Something was wrong. My body shook as I walked upstairs. Was I going back to jail? Had something happened to someone? When we turned the corner, my mom and Uncle Todd sat in the meeting room, and I could see that my mom had been crying. Immediately, I knew.

"It's your grandma, Jason. She's gone," my uncle said, taking the lead for my mom. Tears started to stream from my eyes immediately. I thought about the Christmas card I had written, in which I'd tried to make amends and express my sadness at having created so much pain for her. With quivering lips I asked the only thing I could think about in that moment: "Did she read my card?"

My mom could barely speak through her tears. "She couldn't read, Jason, but we read it to her. She understood us. She knew you were finally here, kid. And then she passed."

My body felt warm and my skin tingled as I heard those words. At least I had gotten one thing right with my grandma in the last decade or so.

My grandma Diane had an infectious smile and a loving spirit that transferred to anyone in the room. She was short and round, with a gray-brown grandma perm that fluffed out in a perfect circle around her head. She was so even-keeled, never getting too upset or excited, moving at a slow yet consistent pace in just about everything she did. When we were kids, my siblings and I practically lived on her farm, especially during the summer months. I remember waking up each morning on the floor where we slept and rolling out from under the sheets. The smell of greasy breakfast food got stronger and stronger with each step down the stairs. I'd turn the corner into the kitchen to find Grammie flipping eggs and Spam and buttering toast, all to feed her kids and grandkids. My grandpa would be off to work already—he owned a cement business and was always gone long before sunrise. We spent those days running around outside, hitting rocks into the field, playing our own versions of football and basketball, and building forts with the hay bales in the big red barn across the road. Often, we intentionally pushed Grammie's buttons just for the fun of it. "You just wait," she'd say, "I'm going to tell your grand-father when he gets home." She was too nice to come after us herself—and most of the time, too nice to actually tell Grandpa about our shenanigans. There was a bit of a rasp to her voice, and she could get loud when she needed to—usually to yell at one of my uncles, who seemed more like cousins, being the same age as us. But her loving and generous ways always won out. She made sure we had everything we needed. That house was a space for fun, a place of release, and a home—all things I struggled to find anywhere else. Grammie was one of the only people who ever made me feel safe. I always knew she had my back.

And now she was gone.

I thought back to the last time I had seen her. It was just a year and a half prior, at the intervention my family had staged. Before I left the house, she was the last family member to take a turn at talking to me. By the time she made it next to me on the couch, I was exhausted from days of partying and an hour of angrily refuting every point my family made about my addiction. But something about Grandma could always make me listen, even if I pretended not to.

With tears running down her cheeks, she placed her hand on my back. "Jason, please do this," she said. "Think of your son—he needs you. He's missing his dad. And the rest of us, we don't see you anymore. We're scared." She paused, and the silence stopped all my thoughts and feelings just long enough for me to hear her next, crushing statement: "I just want my grandson back!"

I held my silence and never looked up. She sniffled, wiped her eyes, and walked away with her head and shoulders drooping. I watched the defeat take over her body. And yet all I could think about was how my family had betrayed me, and how I could make my escape. I stormed out, cursing them all out on my way through the front door, stormed down the stairs, and started the long walk down the gravel road. My relationship with my grandma all but ended that day, and I'd never let that go.

Back at the treatment center, I sat in front of my mom and uncle feeling like the worst human alive. Tears were flowing from all three of us as I thought of the pain I must have caused my grammie. I had lied to my employer during my two-month stint at the group home, claiming I was missing work to visit my sick grandma, but I never made it to see her. And my last words to her were not appropriate to put on paper. All she ever did was love me. And for all those years of work she put in, her reward was being left behind to worry herself sick, and being treated like she was the devil. The truth was, she was an angel. And now I had to face my feelings of intense regret without the normal crutch of drugs and alcohol.

Just before I returned to the isolation of my own room, my mom looked at me and said, "Your grandma's dying wish was granted. You're in treatment, where she always wanted you to be." I turned away in tears, my pain fading into a mix of sadness and remorse, tinged with a bit of satisfaction.

Back in my room, sitting on my bed, my thoughts went to a familiar place. If I could just have one hit of drugs or alcohol, the pain would be relieved. I could almost feel the instant relief that came with my favorite drugs or drinks. I knew stirring up those thoughts wasn't good; if I messed up, I was headed back to jail. And for perhaps the first time in my life when faced with a tragedy, there was a deep part of me that wanted to go through it and actually experience the feelings around my grandma's passing. The only problem was, I didn't know where to turn.

I stood up and walked through my bedroom door and down the hall toward the common area. It was visiting time by then, so the room was filled with other treatment clients hanging with significant others, family, and children. I gravitated toward the chapel at the other end of the wing. I opened the door and stepped in for the first time. The room was small and dimly lit by a chandelier above. There were a couple chairs to the right, and a kneeler straight ahead, facing a cross. There was a calm in that room that I wasn't used to feeling. The air was light, noise was absent, and the simplicity of the room made it easy to pause and reflect. I had no idea what I was doing there, what I was supposed to do, or how others used this room. I walked toward the cross and took the next logical step—kneeling on the hassock. I remembered using one of those when Grandpa used to take us to church. Down on my knees, feeling full of peace but also full of regret, a few tears started down my cheek again. I put my hands together.

"I don't know how this works, if you're out there, or what I'm supposed to do next. I know one thing, only one thing, right now." I paused, gulping as I fought back more tears and pain. Then I let out the most relieving three words I'd used in a long time.

"I need help!"

A simple cry for help in such a complex moment. I knelt there for several more minutes, feeling a certain calm come over me. And then, the response came from somewhere. *It's going to be okay, Jason.* Was it my grandma? Was it this God people talked about? Was it both? Whatever it was, it resonated. I'd never felt that it was going to be okay. Not like that. Not beyond the artificial feelings I'd created with drugs and alcohol. I stood up, my arms and shoulders relaxed, my legs a bit weak, and my head free of the internal noise I was so accustomed to. I backed into the chair behind me and sat in that room for a little while longer, fading from conscious thought and taking in the experience.

> Treatment taught me a lot about drug and alcohol addiction, but most importantly it taught me that I wasn't alone in the fight.

That experience altered the trajectory of my life. Finally, I knew, it really was going to be okay. I went back to that chapel each morning and each night, creating a habit of saying prayers that started as cries for help, and eventually evolved into prayers for others in my life. I was, unbeknownst to myself, developing the first of the most significant tools of my recovery: an acceptance of and reliance upon a power I couldn't define or understand fully. And that was okay, as long it continued to work.

Treatment taught me a lot about drug and alcohol addiction, but most importantly it taught me that I wasn't alone in the fight. For so many years, I simply thought I was defective and didn't stand a chance at living without drugs and alcohol, no matter how hard I tried. But I quickly realized there was a lot more to addiction than my own lack of willpower. I had walked through the doors of that program because I wanted less pain than the jail cell brought. But as I sat through day after day of programming, saw others in treatment and in recovery meetings, I realized there might be a way of living without drugs and alcohol. It didn't make sense to me yet, but I could still watch and believe it was true for others. I took advantage of that experience and developed a sense of gratitude and generosity for having the opportunity to be there. I walked around the unit with my head held higher than it had been in years. I was excited to get up in the morning and didn't want anything to do with going to bed at night. I didn't know what the future held, and I didn't have to. A rare feeling of presence and acceptance filled my days. But I knew I was isolated there, and the real test was yet to come, back out in the community.

"

# WHEN I STARTED COUNTING MY BLESSINGS, MY WHOLE LIFE TURNED AROUND.

WILLIE NELSON

# CHAPTER 11

# FINDING GRATITUDE

After my twenty-eight-day stay in that program, a judge granted me permission to go to Rochester, Minnesota, to live in a halfway house. My uncle Todd drove me up the interstate, about a forty-five-minute drive. The halfway house was a four-story home that held thirty beds, all filled with guys in similar positions. I would be staying on the third floor, in a spacious, wide-open room with three other men. My bed was directly in front of the doorway, jammed up against the wall on the long side, with a partition behind the head of the bed.

I awoke after my first night in that bed to a cold, January morning with darkness filling the room. One of the guys across the way was snoring loudly; the other seemed to sleep right through it. I reached for my CD player and grabbed a mix someone in treatment had made for me. Pulling the headphones over my ears, I turned to song number two, "Grenade" by Bruno Mars. I had listened to that song often when I was using. When I first heard certain songs, like this one, in treatment, I felt a sense of deep association to using and had to fight through those feelings to learn to associate the music with something new. I lay on my back, staring wide-eyed at the ceiling, as the song started. I could hear it, but something else was happening, too. I began to *feel* the song. The sound was soft, but the piano keys felt like they were ringing inside my body, the drums filled my head with beat after beat, and Bruno's pure and heartfelt voice lifted my spirit and energy. Nothing else really mattered in that moment. The music was giving me life. It was my first conscious experience of connecting to and feeling music, from my ears to my soul. I was fully present and in tune with the moment. I was alive in all three dimensions—spiritual, mental, and physical—and all three were in tune with each other. *Is this what life feels like?* I got out of bed that morning excited to start getting my life back together. I needed to find work, get my license, order a social security card, and much more. I had a lot to clean up and I knew it was going to be a challenge, one I had to accept and move through, but I was ready. My new shot at life was off to a good start.

In the end, the house in Rochester turned out not to be a great fit. After witnessing some drug dealing in the house and having some rocky incidents with a local woman I had met in treatment, I knew it was time to get out of there. I was granted permission to transfer to another halfway house in Owatonna. The Owatonna building was much larger than the Rochester house, and housed half as many men. I would be rooming with two older gentlemen. After a quick intake process, I met my counselor, Ron. He was an older guy who, absent a long beard and a big red suit, reminded me of Santa Claus. He had a round shape, long white hair, and glasses, through which he squinted as he talked. He stopped into my room after I had settled in. "I'm Ron, and I'll be your counselor. Here's a journal—why don't you write in this tonight and bring it to me tomorrow, and we can talk some more?" I gladly accepted his offer, unpacked my belongings, and laid on my new bed, smiling with a newfound feeling of gratitude. Finally, I really felt like I was home.

...

A few weeks after I made it to the new halfway house, I took a short walk to my cousin Scott's house. He lived just a few blocks from the halfway house. I opened the front door and headed to the stairs. I took one step down and was immediately overwhelmed with a familiar smell. The draft of marijuana wafting to the top of the stairs was powerful and triggered an immediate craving. Anxiously, I continued down the stairs and saw Scott sitting next to my brother, the pot pipe being passed around. I stood like a deer in headlights, and the look of shock and uncertainty on my face had to be apparent. It seemed like the seconds were minutes, and minutes were hours, as my thoughts paralyzed me. *Would I smoke? What would happen to me if I did?* The temptation was strong, and the opportunity was only feet away, but this time, I had the wherewithal to ask those questions. That had never happened before. My body was tense, my hands trembling, and my mouth started to dry up. I cleared my throat.

"Sorry, I have to run, I can't go back with any kind of smell on me," I mumbled, then I turned and got up the stairs as quickly as I could without looking obvious. "I'll come back tomorrow!" Outside, I speed-walked back toward the halfway house. With some of the tension relieved, my hands trembled even more, sweat formed on my forehead, and my thoughts raced faster than the Daytona 500 winner on the last lap of the race. I knew it was going to be awhile before I went back, and I needed to avoid those situations completely. I had escaped my first real danger in sobriety.

Not too long after that first sober experience around drugs, I went to a college graduation party for my uncle Shane. I was still newly sober, and I knew most people in attendance would be drinking, but I wanted to be there for a few reasons. My uncle was a big part of my life, and it had only been a few months since his mom, my grammie Diane, had passed away. But most of all, it was an opportunity to get together with my son. I had been almost completely out of his life for the better part of four years, and I was committed to doing everything I could to repair that relationship. Getting to know him and mending the damage I had done was going to be a tall order, though. He was already five years old and had little familiarity with me.

When I saw him walk through the door, my heart leaped with a new kind of happiness. I was proud to see what a handsome little boy he had become. He was dressed nicely for the party, with white shoes, neat blue jeans, and a button-down long-sleeve shirt. His hair was spiked in the front, and he had an infectious dimpled smile; his presence was undeniable. I knew

I had to take the relationship slowly, so I settled for a high-five hello. My son was very energetic, but also reserved and shy until he was comfortable in a setting. As we hung out and celebrated my uncle, I felt us growing a little bit closer to each other throughout the evening. I was so thankful for the opportunity to spend time with him again. He was a big reason I wanted to stay sober and on the right track; I wanted to give him what I knew I had missed out on for so long. I knew I faced an uphill climb—it wasn't like everything I had done, or not done, could just be forgotten. Though he was only five, he was smart enough to understand who had been there and who hadn't. Over the next several years, our relationship fluctuated, but through it all, I knew there was one commitment I could make in the matter— to continue doing everything I could to be part of his life, no matter the results. Recovery taught me that it's not about the outcome; it's about doing my part, independent of anyone else's efforts. I knew I had to keep fighting the good fight for that relationship in the hopes that someday it would pay off.

...

Local recovery meetings at the Alano Club were conveniently located right next door to the halfway house, so I went often, sometimes three times per day. I sat in the back, observing the others from a distance and listening to what they shared. I had a hard time imagining my life without drugs and alcohol forever—it was hard to envision how I could be happy with such an existence—but I could see that others had found a way. At twenty-four, while all my old high school buddies were out partying and "living life," I sat alone at the halfway house on weekends, electing not to endanger my sobriety by going out with old friends or family. Most of the people I'd met in recovery were much older than me, and as I sat drinking coffee with them and learning about responsibility, I wondered what I was going to do with my life. It felt boring and glum, but I kept hearing, "Don't quit before the miracle happens!" I didn't know what the miracle was, but I stayed open to seeing this recovery thing through for a bit. My only other option was jail, and I couldn't go back.

I started working the twelve steps of recovery, which are similar across groups for drugs, alcohol, and other addictions. The work was grueling and embarrassing at times. For the better part of a dozen years, I had lied, stolen, cheated, and harmed a *lot* of people, including many who were close to me. Digging that up and sharing what I had done took grit and required a desperation that could only come from the pain and suffering of addiction. Little by little, I began to mold the beginning of a lifestyle that held a glimmer of hope. I still had a hard time comprehending the possibilities of recovery, but I saw how others had made their possibilities realities. If nothing else, I believed that others believed. And then I met a man who would alter how I moved forward in recovery, and eventually, in life.

I made my way into the mix a little more in recovery meetings, sitting on the corner of the main square of tables and chairs. Next to me, on the other side, sat a shorter, older man with glasses, a full goatee in all shades of gray, and thinning hair combed back over his head. I hadn't seen him there before. He spoke in a very deep and monotone voice about how important it was to welcome new people to recovery. He explained that in his early days, he would never have come back without the welcome he felt from a few others in the room. What he was saying really resonated with me. I was new to the meetings myself and was always slow to assimilate and get comfortable with new people, but as he shared his similar experience, I settled into my chair a little more. *Maybe I could ask him to be my sponsor*, I thought. After the meeting, we stood up and he introduced himself before I could sneak away, which was my usual move. "I'm Steve," he said. After we talked for a bit, I built up the courage to ask him to be my sponsor, the fancy title most recovery programs gave to a mentor. He told me he was a long-haul trucker, so was gone most weeks and only home on weekends, but he agreed to give it a shot.

. . .

I sat across from Steve at a wooden table in the halfway house's basement dining room. There were no windows, just two long and two short tables forming the rectangle where we ate our dinner. Steve started telling me a bit about his life, especially his struggles with alcohol and drugs, and it was enough to get me started sharing some of my own "junk" that was weighing me down. Just thirty minutes into the conversation with my new sponsor, I already felt more comfortable sharing my troubles with him than I did with family and longtime friends.

That was how recovery worked, I learned—one person's open-ness could open the door for another person to share in return. I told Steve about my undesirable legal situation. I was on a furlough from jail, which meant I'd need to return pending the results of my next court date. "Well, we're here to face all our consequences, and it's time to pay our dues," he said.

*Who is this jerk?* I thought. I expected him to tell me it was going to be okay and that I didn't belong in jail. But he wasn't like that. He was frank, direct, and cared more about what it took to get and stay sober than he did about my feelings. And so I listened. He had lived a life that resembled mine in a lot of ways, and it was easy to see that now he was doing pretty well. That opened me to hearing and following what he said. And besides, I didn't have any other solutions myself. After twenty-four years of proof that my way wasn't working, I had every reason to shut up and listen, so I did.

. . .

Back at the halfway house after a long day out, I spotted some-thing out of the corner of my eye as I walked through my bedroom door. Someone had left a piece of paper on my bed that looked like it had been ripped from a booklet of some sort. There was an exercise outlined on the paper: Create a list of one hundred things you're grateful for, each day until you feel a significant change take place. It was branded with a logo: "The Secret." I knew immediately where it had come from—Jody, the director of the halfway house. She had recently shared a documentary with me called *The Secret*, which, though a bit strange and cheesy, had piqued my interest. It emphasized our ability to attract desirable outcomes simply by stating them as fact before they happen. I sat down with the piece of paper in hand, and I reached back to my dresser top to grab my notebook and a pen. One hundred things to be grateful for? Heck, I didn't imagine I could think of one hundred things, period! I started with the easy things—a new chance at life, my son, my sobriety, freedom—and then transitioned to characteristics of myself that I appreciated. About fifty items in, I started struggling to find things to add to the paper. I stared around that room, looking for ideas. Ah, yes—toothpaste! I tried to imagine life without toothpaste and couldn't help but think about how bad it would be to be in proximity to others after nights of mouth-wide-open sleep. Lights! Life would be impossible, and a lot less safe, without them. And heat—we Minnesotans would freeze to death, literally, without it. It took me an hour to think of those first hundred things to be thankful for. After a few days, I quickly realized I was looking at and for things that were taken for granted entirely too often. As I came up with new items to add, I thought about each one and what life would be like without it. And that's when one of the most foundational principles and practices of my life—gratitude—became a paramount guide for all that I do. Shortly thereafter, I wrote a long journal entry to my counselor that expressed my sincere gratitude for the place where I found myself. I received one of the one-liners he was known for in reply: *If you stay grateful, you'll stay sober.*

...

It had finally arrived—my day in front of the judge. I had hardly slept the night before, tossing and turning as I played out all the possible scenarios. Was I going back to jail? I had done so much work in my first five months of sobriety, but anxiety and worry still plagued most days. My counselor reassured me I had done everything I could have, and reminded me that if the judge really wanted me locked up for a while, he wouldn't have let me go to treatment at all. That helped quell the anxiety, but it was still hard to face the fact that the outcome was out of my control. My fate and all the power to determine my future was in the hands of three people: the prosecutor, my probation officer, and, ultimately, the judge.

Sunlight poured in through the windows on the east side of the building and lit up the hallway outside the court room. My probation officer, a short woman in her forties, approached me in the corner with what felt like a half-sincere smile. She asked how I was and made a little small talk before the doors to the court room swung open.

"All parties in the matter of Jason Lennox, please enter now," the court officer announced. I walked in with my public defender, followed by my probation officer. The prosecutor came from a side door and joined the probation officer. The room was cold and silent, and the air felt incredibly heavy. Waiting for the judge to come through the door, I sat with a familiar feeling of uncertainty and fear. My body tensed up, and I prepared to do and say whatever it took to stay out of jail that day.

"Your Honor, I've spoken at length with Ms. Wolfe, Mr. Lennox's probation officer, and we give accolades to Mr. Lennox for the clear progress he's made in the last several months," the prosecutor opened. "It is because of the evident attempt at a new way of life that we aren't going to recommend he return to jail; instead, we recommend a thirty-day jail sentence that he will not have to serve if he completes his current treatment."

My shoulders relaxed a little and my breath slowed just a bit as I realized I might remain a free man.

"However," the prosecutor continued, "we don't think Mr. Lennox can leave without some consequence for his actions. He has failed, over and over, to obey the orders of this court and his probation officer. He ran from those orders for nearly a year, and was only caught after a 911 call revealed an arrest warrant. We therefore recommend the felony drug charge remain in his criminal record, revoking his stay of adjudication."

This was a crushing blow. My previous agreement would have wiped that felony from my record as long as I stayed out of trouble, and that was in jeopardy now. The judge, a bald man with glasses pushed to the bottom of his nose, looked down and took notes, then directly at me and asked, "Mr. Lennox, do you have anything you wish to say for yourself?"

Like a flash of lightning, all the moments in which I had sat in front of judges flooded into my thoughts. Usually, I denied the claims against me and lied for as long as I could, pleading for forgiveness only when I was cornered and found out. But on this day, recovery came out in a surprising way. I took a few deep breaths and let the weight of the world fall off my shoulders, and with a shaky voice and quivering lips, I said something that surprised even me.

"Your Honor, you know better than anyone what that felony does to my future. I feel like I've gained an understanding of why I did what I did in the past and truly feel like I have a path in front of me that leads to a new life. But I'm not here to ask for any more chances, to tell any more lies, or to convince you to change your mind. I've been given so many opportunities by you all, and I understand those opportunities aren't unending. I'm here to truly own my actions and finally accept the consequences, whatever they may be."

My body was still shaking, but it felt fifty pounds lighter. It was the greatest moment of authenticity of my life. I had finally taken full responsibility for my actions, and that unexpected choice was met with an equally surprising response from the judge.

"All, I am not inclined to mar Mr. Lennox's future quite yet. I am ordering you, Mr. Lennox, to a thirty-day sentence in the detention center in the event you do not complete your treatment. Upon successful completion of treatment, you will be free to go, following the orders of your probation officer for the remainder of your probation period. Use this opportunity, wisely, Mr. Lennox, and keep up the good work."

I was astonished at the response and overwhelmed with gratitude. I walked out of the courthouse that day knowing if I could find a way to sustain my new way of life, I would never have to be locked up again. The running, the worrying, the fighting—it was all over. The sincerity with which I spoke that day created space for me to sense all the things I'd missed out on most days. As I walked back to the halfway house about a mile away, I was present to life in a whole new way. I smelled the fresh scent of newly cut grass, saw the brightness of the blue sky, heard the swishing of the rivers flowing under each bridge I walked over, and felt the aliveness of the spring air. I knew in that moment what life was all about. Finally, I moved beyond mere hope for survival, toward the hope for a meaningful life.

...

I had been in some sort of facility—jail, inpatient treatment, or the halfway house—for about six months when my counselor told me that the funding had run out. My treatment was being paid for through the county because I had no insurance, and time was up. I had been searching for a couple months for a place of my own, but my applications were denied one after another. My criminal and financial histories were too risky and created significant barriers for me. I was left with two choices— return to a home that would expose me to regular drug and alcohol use, or accept my sponsor's gracious offer to stay in his basement for a while. What I really wanted was some peace and space to call my own, but at the eleventh hour, I made the call to my sponsor and asked if he'd still have me. The next day, he came with a truck to load up the few belongings I had.

As I walked out of the halfway house for the last time, I turned back to the cream-colored brick building and reflected on all the things I had learned and accomplished there. It had been a safe place I knew I could always come back to. Getting out into the real world, where being monitored would not be part of my routine, was going to be very different. That was scary, and so was going to live with a couple I had only known for a few months. I didn't know what to expect in this next phase, but I soon found an unexpected source of comfort in my new hosts.

The basement at Steve's house was undergoing some work, as one of the cats had peed all over the carpet. The smell of cat urine was strong, mingled with the mustiness that came with a damp basement. At the bottom of the stairs, I was met by my sponsor's wife, Deb, a short woman with dark, wavy hair down to her shoulders. She wore glasses and had a beauty mark above the left side of her mouth. Deb reached down from the first stair and pulled me in for a hug, squeezing tightly.

"Welcome home," she said. Those two words and that hug instantly relieved the incredible discomfort I'd had about staying there, and opened the door to what would turn out to be a life-changing relationship.

Later that night, as I lay in my bed in the basement, I wondered what Deb and Steve must have been thinking. I reflected on all the things I'd done to others over the years, all the stealing, lying, cheating, and betraying. It seemed crazy that a family like this, seemingly so well put together, would be placed in my path, and more importantly, would take a chance on a loser like me. Sure, I had done some good things over the past six months, but I had also spent twelve years doing damage to others. I thanked the power I had started to rely on for the shelter, food, and safety that Steve and Deb's house was already

146

providing. But as important as it was to have a safe environ-ment to live in, I also needed a new outlook on life; I needed to learn what a life of sobriety would look like. I still questioned where the fun would be. What would I do on weekends? What would I do during holiday seasons? I had no idea. But Steve and Deb did. With them, I went to sober parties and hung out with a lot of fun, sober people. They lived a full life, and I couldn't help but pay attention to all the things they did along the way. The ideas of selflessness and generosity shone through in all that they did, and in all that they taught me to do.

That summer, I quit my construction job building con-crete foundations and took my first huge leap of blind faith in recovery—I made a quick decision to go back to school. I didn't know how I'd earn money or if I'd even make it in school, but I knew I didn't want to work construction forever. I hadn't been to school since high school, about six years prior, aside from a few days' attempt at community college when I was twenty-one. And even in high school, I had spent the last several years simply doing the minimum work needed to keep me in good standing for sports. I was excited and scared at the same time. As it turned out, school was easier than I thought it would be now that I was sober and motivated to do well. It brought a new routine and purpose to my life, a life that was quickly growing in meaning, value, and hope.

> **THE BEST TIME TO PLANT A TREE WAS 20 YEARS AGO. THE SECOND BEST TIME IS NOW.**

UNKNOWN

# CHAPTER 12

# THE SEED

Driving down a winding country road on a hot day earlier that summer, Steve had asked me how I was feeling about recovery. I told him I felt great—I had been attending a lot of meetings, doing a lot of service work, and having fun playing softball on weekends. With my life filling up, I had started to see possibility in a future without drugs and alcohol.

"I think you're ready to sponsor others in recovery," he said.

I paused. "In treatment, they told me to find a sponsor with two years of sobriety, so I don't think I'm ready for that yet," I told him. I'll never forget what he said next.

"I don't care what treatment said. The recovery literature tells us when we have an experience to share with the next person, we do it. If you wait until you have two years of sobriety to serve others, you won't see two years of sobriety."

Chills ran through my body, pausing all the racket of my usual thoughts, emotions, and feelings. That hit home. I knew I needed to listen. It was in that moment that the seed of a new idea was planted: My sobriety depended on supporting the sobriety of those around me. And on an even deeper plane, the value of my life was ultimately going to be measured by the value I provided in others' lives. It was time to get to work, and I was ready.

I started sponsoring others, leading recovery meetings, and joining committees that planned recovery-related events. Life at home was good, too—I felt supported by Deb and Steve, who I had begun to refer to as "Ma" and "Pa," and I was hoping to finish my two-year degree from their home. But soon, Ma and Pa pushed me toward the next fork in the road of my life. They thought it was time for me to find my own place to live, and take on the next level of responsibility. It was a scary prospect—financially, my own place was going to be a lot more expensive. I was in school full-time and had no source of income. But I started looking, and eventually found an apartment manager willing to bypass my background flaws and give me a chance. The day she called and told me they accepted my application, I was elated and shared the great news with Ma and Pa. I was excited to finally have my own space, but I knew it wasn't going to be easy. Thankfully, I had recovery meetings to share in. The people who had been around for a while always said, "Just do the next right thing, and the rest will work out." *Easy for them to say*, I thought. I now realize, it was easy for them to say, because they knew. But I didn't, not yet.

As fear crept in amid all the new responsibilities I had taken on, brief thoughts of drugs and alcohol began to creep back in, too. Those brief thoughts would turn into intense memories of highs playing through in my head. Anxious about caring for my own place, paying bills, and the uncertainty of life in general, I had the thought that

## My sobriety depended on supporting the sobriety of those around me.

using would make it all go away. I knew that was true—and I knew it would ruin my life. Each day I faced the question of which thought would hold more weight. I was in a dangerous position, swaying from the comfort I knew drugs and alcohol always provided, to the guilt and shame I could already feel on the other side of that comfort. I felt like I couldn't share those doubts with anyone. Everyone thought I was doing so well, and I couldn't jeopardize that picture. At ten months sober, I was confused, and starting to feel as badly as I had in active addiction.

It was in this state that I found myself sitting in a Walmart parking lot one warm October Sunday evening, staring at the sun through my front windshield. I wasn't even sure why I was there. My head felt like it was beating heavily and might explode at any minute. My stomach was in knots. I sat holding the warm steering wheel of my white Oldsmobile, debating my next steps. I wanted to reach out for some drugs, but I was too ashamed to ask anyone I used to hang with. I had come so far, and I didn't want to reveal myself as someone who was giving up on sobriety. And besides, I knew what waited on the other side of that decision. I thought about my life and what value was left in it. Tears pooled in my eyes. The sunlight blurred, and I dropped my head into the palms of my hands, aggressively rubbing the tears out. The pain was overpowering, and helplessness sunk me into my seat. I thought about suicide. I didn't want to hold all these feelings in anymore, and I couldn't go back. All the pain I had felt in my active addiction piled onto the pain I felt in that moment. I thought back to the little boy with a knife to his chest and wondered why he didn't just follow through. It would have saved a lot of trouble. I couldn't even get sobriety right. And I knew I wouldn't get a relapse right.

In a matter of weeks, I had moved from a satisfying life to a jumping-off point, as recovery likes to call it, where I couldn't imagine surviving the pain of a relapse, and I couldn't imagine living without drugs and alcohol. Both options brought too much discomfort to bear. I was done. Until, suddenly, a third option occurred to me.

From some unknown power, a new thought came to my mind that was unlike the rest. *What about that Jay guy I hung with last night?* I had known Jay for a little while; we attended some of the same meetings and he was part of the recovery group my sponsor hung with. I listened to him in meetings a lot, where he always said, "God is doing for me what I couldn't do for myself." While it was hard to comprehend, I always felt the conviction and truth in that statement—I believed that he believed it, and I held on to that. We had all gone out the previous night for dinner before a meeting, and I had stopped at Jay's house later to drop off leftover food, as he had been on a bike and couldn't carry it. As fate would have it, that brought him to the front of my mind that night, and I picked up the phone, trembling, and scrolled to find his name. When he answered, I could hardly contain myself. I let him know I needed help fast, that I was in a bad spot mentally. He invited me over; I accepted before he had even gotten the invitation out.

I drove across town as quickly as I could, and when I arrived, I frantically explained where my head was at. Shame prevented me from fully disclosing my thoughts around suicide, but thankfully I was able to open up enough to express the nature of my emotional state. My senses heightened, I was nervous and scared of what my future looked like. Jay listened intently from his chair, waiting for small moments to interject. Short and muscular, with subtly blond hair, he had a quiet yet firm voice, and his presence could calm an entire room. Finally, he scooted to the front of his chair and said confidently, "Let's just get to work on these twelve steps of recovery. It will get better, man."

I had started on those twelve steps twice before, but I hadn't finished the first time and had left some key secrets out the second time. I agreed to go through the steps again, this time feeling ready to fully take on the work. I was tired of sharing, so intimately and vulnerably, the darkest parts of my life with someone and not seeing lasting results.

Jay and I went to work, reading through the steps and principles of recovery literature that have turned hundreds of thousands, maybe millions, of people struggling with addiction into healthy and productive beings. When I left Jay's house that evening, I felt some relief, gratitude, and a glimmer of hope for something different. Over the coming days, I worked through the steps for the third time. I felt a desperation to get it right that I had never experienced before, knowing very well that I might never again find the courage to reach out like I had that fateful Sunday evening. I acted as if this was my last chance at success, and because of that, I gave it my all. For the first time, I was determined to leave nothing out. There were three sections to the packet that sat on my dresser—wrongdoings, fears, and resentments. I dedicated a few days to each one, praying for wisdom in the process each day. As soon as names, places, people, and things would come to my mind, no matter how big or small, they would land on my paper. It was the most thorough examination of my life I'd ever taken part in. The night before I planned to meet Jay for what religion considered "confession," I stared at my ceiling, thinking about how I would share. I was scared, but I was even more desperate. I prayed that night for the courage to let it all out, once and for all.

The next day, I left my apartment for Jay's place, ready to unleash what felt like hundreds of pounds of weight. I accepted a cup of coffee and poured in some French vanilla creamer, and we headed for his living room. After a few short minutes of small talk, we got down to business. We walked through every detail I had written down—all the people I had harmed, all the things I was fearful of, and all the people and circumstances I was mad at. The packet was six pages long, and we unpacked one page after another over the next few hours. It was emotional, exhausting, and tiring. Finally, we reached the end. There was nothing left on my paper.

"Is there anything else you haven't shared?" Jay asked.

My stomach sank. There were two things I hadn't been able to put to paper. One of them was too embarrassing to talk about, and the other could get me into a lot of legal trouble, as I had done some serious damage to someone's property. Just as I had in my last attempt at this practice, I froze and told him no.

As if Jay knew what was happening inside me, he said, "I remember when I was sharing my life with someone, too, there were a few things I just couldn't get myself to share. After the person shared similar things with me, I felt safe enough to open up about what I thought were the darkest secrets I had."

When Jay then shared his own deepest secrets with me, I was astonished to learn that one of them was practically the same as the secret I'd been holding in. The door was open, and I walked through. For the first time ever, I let both secrets out. Afterward, Jay hugged me and asked me if we could pray together. The relief I felt on that couch was immense. I stood up from that prayer feeling both exhausted and rejuvenated at the same time. I knew I was one large step closer to finishing this work.

The next step—making right the wrongs I had done to others—was going to require a new kind of authenticity and vulnerability. It might not require digging as deep as what I had just endured, but I knew I would need to let myself be authentic and vulnerable over and over and over again. I had harmed a lot of people. I assumed some of them would never entertain the thought of hearing me out, but that wasn't up to me. The only thing I could control was making the attempt.

First up on my list was an old landlord from Claremont. Dean was a kind and pleasant older man, tall and skinny with gray hair, who owned the building I used to live in. I'd convinced him to let me manage the building, and he gave me chance after chance when I wouldn't come through with my end of the agreement. I took all the rent in from others in the building, but never paid Dean any of the rent I owed him. I used to hide in that building for days, coming and going as sneakily as I could, knowing the day the locks would be changed was inevitable. I accumulated thousands of dollars of debt before I left town and made my way back to Owatonna. A year and a half later, I had tried to reach out, leaving him multiple messages, but I never heard back. I had no clue how I'd pay him back, but I wanted to take responsibility for my actions and come up with some plan to repair the damage I'd done. Now, as I worked my way through the twelve steps again, I was about to experience the way in which the spirit of this world worked.

After a Sunday night recovery meeting for newcomers that I regularly attended, under a November sky full of shining stars, I was approached by a man named Don. Don was in his forties, with dark hair, a medium build, and an anxious disposition that was clear in his shaking hands, quivering lips, and fumbled sentences.

"I really loved what you had to say," he complimented me. "I'm looking for a sponsor and was wondering if you'd be mine?"

I hesitated, knowing I was in the middle of some tough stuff myself, but ultimately agreed to help him. As I asked a little more about him, I quickly realized that his office was in Dean's building in Claremont. I couldn't believe it! I told Don a little bit about my past and asked him to have Dean call me.

"I just want to repay my debts, I'm not looking for anything else," I assured him. Don agreed to pass the message along. Just a couple days later, he got back to me and told me Dean was willing to have me work on the building to pay off my debt. It was the perfect scenario, considering I had no money with which to pay him.

With the days shortening and sunset happening earlier each day, I went to work, often bringing along men from the halfway house I had lived in, both to give them some income and to help speed the process along. The roof needed to be replaced, and there were five layers of roofing to tear up. The work was grueling, but I found comfort in it, knowing I was trying to make right this tremendous wrong I'd done. I remember standing on that roof, staring off into the sunset to the west, breathing in the crisp and cold fall air, and experiencing an emptiness that I hadn't felt before. It wasn't a bad emptiness—instead, it felt like an openness in all the pathways of my body, allowing my feelings and thoughts to flow freely. There was something happening that was new to me, something I couldn't particularly put my finger on. But I didn't need to—just feeling it was enough.

After a couple weeks, I was shocked when Dean cut me a check for the work I was doing. It didn't make sense—the agreement was that I'd work off my debt, there wasn't supposed to be any money involved. I did all I could to reject the offer, but all Dean said was, "Just keep doing the right thing and that'll be payment enough." As I drove home that night on some of the same roads that I associated with the most painful times in my life, I felt a few tears trickle down. I understood that while I might not ever feel worthy of this generosity, I could accept the grace and pass it on someday when I was in a more able position. I was humbled, grateful, and determined to do right by all the others I needed to. Just a month or so removed from thoughts of suicide, I was moving into a new phase of life—one that would make or break my long-term plans for sobriety.

...

Just after the one-year anniversary of my sobriety, I stood in Dean's building after a day of work and stared at the wooden wall of the long, dark hallway, tears forming in my eyes. Out the window, large snowflakes drifted slowly from the sky toward the ground. I thought back to all the parties in that apartment, and remembered intensely all the sadness and despair I had felt there. This was the place where my worst days of addiction were lived. I wondered how I had gotten here. A little over a year after my near-fatal overdose, I stood in the same space that had almost taken me down.

**Just one year into recovery, I felt a sense of victory that only living the right life could bring.**

I thought about the recovery celebration coming later that night, and especially that my grandpa was coming. My grandma's loss was still heavy on my heart, and having my grandpa come to a recovery meeting, something I never imagined he'd do, was a step toward healing from losing her. He represented her, and I wanted them both to be proud. I had managed to outlast the evils of addiction for a whole year. In a moment of the most intense gratitude I'd ever experienced, everything went silent, and the tears started streaming. I knew the fight was over, finally. My obsessive thoughts about drugs and alcohol were gone. I was going to make it, no matter what happened. Just one year into recovery, I felt a sense of victory that only living the right life could bring. The principles I'd been living by were working, and I knew I'd never let them go. Perhaps unconsciously, from that moment on, I understood that my new job was to share my victory with as many people as possible.

...

Recovery was creating opportunities I wasn't accustomed to, and I started to believe those guys who always said, "Just do the next right thing." It seemed like every challenge I faced was met with opportunity. As the work on my old building concluded, my bills were starting to pile up, and I knew I needed a more consistent income. I started looking for work anywhere I could, applying at grocery stores, clothing stores, even gas stations. One after another, the rejections came in. Some places never called back; others at least gave a reason why they weren't interested. At one gas station, I was told, "Mr. Lennox, we're sorry, but your experience doesn't fit what we are looking for." *You've got to be kidding me*, I thought. *It's a gas station clerk job, there is no experience needed.* I realized that my recovery didn't mean the same thing to everyone else that it did to me—just because I had gotten my act together didn't mean the rest of the world was suddenly ready to hand me the keys to the Lamborghini. I'd hoped they would at least let me into the station wagon, though. With every rejection I received, I knew I had two choices—I could fall into a state of self-pity, or tell myself those companies were the unfortunate ones, and that eventually I'd make a real difference for the one that took a chance. I held my head high and gained a confidence I hadn't had since high school.

After months of searching, a buddy helped me land a job at the local country club. It paid minimum wage—just $7.25 per hour at the time—but it was a very flexible job, so I could work around my school hours. And the work was very peaceful much of the time. Mowing a golf course early in the morning, sitting on a mini tractor listening to music, and having a lot of fun with coworkers who were also in recovery was worth the lower pay. I later landed another minimum-wage job working evenings and sleeping overnights at a group home. Mercifully, after my overdose the state had opted not to report my drug use at the group home where I used to work. The neglect and on-site drug use I'd engaged in there was more than enough to slap me with a label that would have prevented me from ever seeking another human services job, so I knew that getting back into the field of helping others was nothing short of a miracle for me. I wasn't going to ruin it this time.

**"**

# THE OPPOSITE OF ADDICTION IS NOT SOBRIETY. IT IS HUMAN CONNECTION.

JOHANN HARI

# CHAPTER 13

# A NEW CALLING

The road to recovery is never a straight line. In 2014, I had thankfully already started seeing a therapist to dig into the unaddressed issues of my childhood when I found out I would need to have a major reconstructive knee surgery. The surgery isolated me at home for many weeks, and it required prescription pills that brought me back to an eerily familiar place. It thrust me into a mental health crisis, so during one of our sessions a couple weeks after surgery, my therapist recommended that I stay with Ma and Pa until I was in a more stable state of mind. Luckily, I was still there when I got a devastating call from my brother John.

By the time I had hung up the phone, I was lying on Ma's vinyl dining room floor, broken and crying aloud. There was a dog on each side, licking my face—they knew something was terribly wrong. They were right. John had just called to tell me my cousin Scott had died in a motorcycle crash that morning.

Scott had been my idol growing up. He was six years older than me, and I followed in his footsteps, wanting to be just like him. I remember one year, Scott started his own baseball team, the Raptors, and they practiced just down the road from my childhood home in an open grass field behind a gas station. I showed up to watch every practice, dreaming of the day I could be out there playing. My dedication paid off the day Scott gave me a shirt to use as a blank slate for my jersey. I was maybe eight or nine years old. Thrilled, I went home and found a permanent marker. I drew the number twenty-nine and my last name on the back side of the shirt and held it up to assess my work. The two was twice the size of the nine, and my name was slanting down to the right. Though I was slightly embarrassed by the job I'd done, I brought the jersey back the next day and felt proud to be part of the team. Scott took one look at my handiwork and laughed. "We don't use marker; we use spray paint. I'll make another one for you, kid," he promised. I watched in awe as he threw and hit the ball as hard as anyone I'd ever seen. He was the first person I ever really wanted to be like.

In my adult years, Scott took me in and helped me straighten up a bit a few times. He knew the struggle of addiction personally, and after I sobered up, he always told me how proud he was of me. But in the past few years, we'd lost touch as he moved to Colorado to spend more time with his sister, Candice. He'd come back from time to time and we'd see each other for the odd summer gathering or family get-together, but we had lost regular contact. Scott was one of the key influencers of my life, and his loss absolutely crushed me. As the shock settled, regret started to sink in. I wished I had spent more time with him, checked in with him more, and most of all let him know how much he meant to me. Regret hit me hard. I'd spent a lot of time working to clean up of all the messes I'd made, repairing the things I'd done that I shouldn't have. But as it turned out, that was only one side of regret. When Scott died, I learned the hard way that the other side was all the things I could have and should have done, but hadn't.

A couple days after his death, I headed back home. In the darkness of my windowless living room, I sat in my chair and prepared a memorial video for Scott. As I worked, I reflected on what I had learned in grieving for Scott. If I couldn't go back in time and do right by him before he left the world, I could still do the next best thing. From that moment, I promised myself I would dedicate my time and energy to family above all else.

...

By 2014, I was succeeding in school, loving both my jobs, and developing a rock-solid recovery network. I had begun to experience gratification and the kind of balance in life that I thought most "normal" people probably experienced, with the right combination of work, school, fun, and rest. It had taken me twenty-six years to climb out of the valley and get back to the baseline of life. But far from being discouraged by that, I knew the uphill climb I'd traversed gave me a unique opportunity to make a powerful difference in the world. I had already begun to tell my story in one-on-one settings and at recovery meetings and treatment centers. I was especially interested in supporting

Fountain Centers, the treatment center where it had all started for me, so I scheduled a meeting with an outreach staff member from the program named Jenine. One Thursday when I had the day off, I drove down to Albert Lea to meet with her. Jenine had short brown hair and an infectious smile and personality. After talking for a bit, she set me up to come back as a regular speaker each month, where I could share my personal story and message of hope. As it turned out, Jenine had recently spoken at my old high school and was scheduled to return the next Tuesday. When she found out I had gone to NRHEG, she looked at me with wide eyes and enthusiastically asked, "What are you doing Tuesday?"

She asked me to join her to share at my old high school, to the entire district of staff, about how traumatic events contributed to addiction. I was overwhelmed by the thought of talking to the entire district, but also honored that she'd asked, so I agreed to a tag-team approach.

As I drove to the high school the following Tuesday, I crossed over the railroad tracks and looked to my right at the park I had hung out in, even slept in, so many times. I looked away. Today was not a day to entertain those thoughts. I pulled into the student parking lot, where a huge sign with the school mascot was flashing messages across the screen. I found a spot near the front of the lot, parked my car, and sat in silence. I closed my eyes, recalling so many years of pain and misery in that town. I was still holding on to some of the grief of having lost all my friends and the life that had seemed so perfect. I opened my eyes. Looking to the western sky, all I could see was gray. I imagined the moment I'd be in front of the crowd, and began to feel vulnerable and afraid. I put my hands together and said a prayer. *Please help me realize my purpose here, and help me tell the truth, no matter how hard it is.*

I walked across the road and up the ramp to the front door, aware of where my fear was coming from. I didn't usually mind public speaking, and hardly flinched when telling my darkest and deepest secrets in crowds, but this was different. In the past, I had always told my story in recovery settings, to people who were just like me, people who understood the tragedy of addiction. But on that day, I was about to share my life with teachers, mentors, even friends turned teachers, who had seen me at my worst. This was as raw as it could ever get, as my nerves made very clear.

I stood by Jenine's side in the front of an open space, facing around seventy-five staff members, coaches, and mentors.

"I think most of you probably know my guest speaker. He's one of your very own, Jason Lennox," she exclaimed. All eyes were on me. It was time to do what I had come to do. As I spilled one story after another, outlining the chronological story of my upbringing, my addiction, and the few years of recovery I had under my belt, I could feel the confusion and frustration around addiction dissipating among the crowd. I watched as my lived experience, shared so transparently and authentically, brought on looks of amazement, tears, and even a few laughs. It was easy to see the surprise and terror on my audience's faces as I shared some of my darkest days, followed by their comforting smiles as I shared about my salvation.

There were many people in that room who had done everything they could to support me. As I spoke, my football coach

167

could hardly look at me directly; his wife couldn't hold back the tears. So many people who had seen my demise were finally able to understand what reality was for me, and that changed their perspectives. They were also able to let go of the *What could I have done differently?* questions and insecurities that many of them had carried for years. They had wanted to help. They had tried to help. They just didn't see immediate results. And as a result, they felt insufficient as teachers, as mentors, as people. But what they did do, along with so many others, was plant the seeds of ideas that would later grow and be remembered. And in my speech that day, they saw the realization of the work they had all done, and felt the gratitude I shared for it. It was an emotional forty-five minutes, maybe the most moving speech I'd ever given, and it would impact me in ways I couldn't yet anticipate. After a bunch of hugs and handshakes, I walked out of my old high school, the place where my life rose and fell so sharply, with an incredible sense of relief and closure. I drove away from New Richland that day knowing, without a doubt, that I had found my greatest talent and passion. I could sense deeply that speaking and writing would be an integral part of my recovery, and more importantly, my life.

...

Before long, the confidence I had in this new direction would get a boost in the most unlikely of places—amid a family tragedy, at my grandfather's funeral.

I had known something was wrong as soon as I saw my mom's call come in. "He's gone." Her voice trembled over the phone.

"What do you mean?" I asked.

"Grandpa, he's gone. I found him in the bathroom," she bawled. I felt a paralysis come over me. It didn't make sense. Grandpa Jim was only seventy-three, and there was nothing seriously wrong with him. Just a couple months prior, his youngest brother, my uncle David, had passed away from cancer. And now, a tragic fall in the shower was all it had taken to yank the center of our family from our lives. My grandpa was gone. I sped to Waseca to be with family, taking the next couple days off work. When I arrived, my mom asked if I would put together a eulogy centered on people's stories and memories of my grandpa. I loved writing, and I was happy to contribute to honoring my grandpa in any way.

Everyone knew Jim, so there were plenty of stories to choose from. My grandpa had been a tall, towering man, with white curly hair and hands and limbs as large as a bear's. His handshake was crippling, and his one-eyed smile would precede bursts of laughter that rang through any room he was in. He commanded a great respect, but in such a gentle way. Grandpa worked hard, played hard, and was the center of attention not just in our family, but in the wider community as well. He was the leader of our family, hosting holidays and weeklong trips up north. Above all, he was known for his character—full of integrity, always giving, never complaining, he was a man who simply did his best, every day of his life. I had always admired him and wanted to be like him.

Now, as my family gathered in the small town of Waldorf,

Minnesota, on a cool August night, I sat in my grandpa's favor-ite recliner. It was closer to a love seat in size, with fabric as soft as a kitten's fur. The cushions enveloped me, and the foot-rest kicked out to the perfect height. I opened my computer and started typing away, putting all the stories together. When I'd finished compiling everyone else's words, I was left with one final addition—my own memory.

It was around 4 a.m. as I sat up in Grandpa's chair to finish the eulogy. The house was silent, the lights were still on, and the windows were open. Out of nowhere, a cool breeze came floating through the dining room, brushing my hair and face, and, just as quickly as it came, it was gone. *Thank you, Grandpa,* I thought. *I got this.*

The next morning, I held my emotions in the best I could, feeling like a loosely twisted-on cap on a shaken-up soda bot-tle, as I read story after story about my grandpa. Some were funny, some were heartwarming, some were heartbreaking. I kept it together through all of them, and finally, with chills running through my body and sweat beads forming on my forehead, I arrived at the last paragraph. I pictured that subtle grin my grandpa always had as I read out the memory of him that I would always treasure.

"It was a typical card party at the old farmhouse, a few years into my sobriety, and I was getting ready to leave. Grandpa had given me his typical goodbye, which included that firm hand-shake and a nice shoulder tap. As I went to pull away, he pulled me in a little closer and said words that will forever echo in my ears: 'Hey, I thank God every day that you're doing what you're doing. You know your grandma would be proud.'"

I continued, "For you, Grandpa, and for you, Grandma, I will continue to do what I'm doing, as will the rest of the Jewison family. We will continue to carry on your legacy of hard work, respect, humility, and love. Though your life may have come suddenly to an end, we will, someday, see you again."

As I stepped back to exit the stage, the crowd burst into applause, as if we were at the end of a stunning performance

> **I was reminded yet again of my purpose on earth—to speak hope into as many people as possible.**

on *American Idol* rather than in the middle of a Catholic church funeral. As my uncles and my mom embraced me and thanked me, a wave of gratitude and love washed over me. I knew I had honored my grandpa in the final minutes of his service, and that the day had helped to bring our family together. It was the most moving experience of my life. I left feeling like I was no longer the one missing out and regretting the losses in life; rather, I was someone who had the privilege of contributing to the memories. I was reminded yet again of my purpose on earth—to speak hope into as many people as possible. My cousin Ben, visiting from Massachusetts, told me something that day I'd never forget: "That thing you did at the podium, you need to find a way to do that in whatever you do. That's a real gift." He was right. It was a gift, and I had to use it in all that I did.

One year to the day after losing my grandpa, my family would suffer another great loss. My grandma Donna, my mom's mom, was one of the few people I had managed to maintain a great relationship throughout my post–high school years. When I got sober and started playing softball, she would pop over on her motorized scooter to watch the games, which were just a couple blocks from her apartment building. Her scooter was equipped with enough animal treats and food for an entire zoo, and she drove around town all day, feeding animals, exploring the town, and enjoying the weather. Eventually, she inherited her own little dog, who would ride on the floor of her scooter. The dog would pop its head up at all the stops, tongue hanging out even from its closed mouth. Those two were a match made in heaven. Grandma would drop in to see me at work or at home, and I couldn't help but chuckle every time I saw her coming. With five-foot flags extending from her scooter, even from a distance she couldn't be missed, and that's how she wanted it.

As Grandma declined in her final days, I was able to spend some quality time just being with her, sitting on her bed, combing her hair, and holding her hand. She would spit out words that didn't make much sense sometimes. One of the last times I heard her talk, she said, "Only the white people. One foot of the blanket . . . the other." I chuckled as I sat in the chair next to her bed, the sun shining in on her grayish, pale skin. "What was that, Grammie?" I asked. She muttered similar words again, her eyes closed and head shaking. I grabbed her hand and she squeezed.

Later that night, as I drove home in the dark, I finally figured out what she had been trying to communicate. It was an old Native American saying: *Only a white man would believe you could cut a foot off the top of a blanket, sew it onto the bottom of the blanket, and be left with a longer blanket.* Even as she faded away, she was doing what Grandma did best—teaching me lessons. I could almost hear her voice saying, "Don't sacrifice time with family today, thinking it will be there tomorrow." I took comfort in knowing I was there with her, doing what I could. The next morning, she passed away, and for maybe the first time in my life, I had the experience of losing a loved one without feeling that I had left anything unspoken or undone. Losing my second grammie brought me comfort around the way I had lost my first. I had finally done it. I had finally found peace.

In the years that followed, I chose to remember Grandma Donna's lesson, prioritizing family above all else. I worked to begin rebuilding a relationship with my son, visiting with him weekly at his grandma's home. Some weeks, he loved hanging out, and some weeks he wanted nothing to do with it. I couldn't blame him; I knew I had caused him unimaginable pain and let him down during the most important years of his life. Remembering the resentment I'd felt toward my own father for his inability to pull his life together and get it right for us, I've always tried to meet my son with understanding, even through the sting of rejection I'd feel when he didn't want to see me. Recovery has taught me that I need to accept my own responsibility and continue to do what I can to maintain the relationship, and over the years, that work has paid off. We may not have had the typical father–son dynamic, but watching Aiden grow

into a young man has been a blessing, and I'm grateful for the way our relationship has continued to evolve.

I also began to travel regularly to spend time with my cousins, and I made a pilgrimage to visit Scott's family in Colorado. I managed to reconnect with my dad's family on the East Coast, who I now visit a few times per year. Through those visits, I've gotten to know my father in ways I never thought possible, all through the beautiful stories and love shared by all my aunties. With them, I feel at home, and I've learned the true essence of love, without bounds and without conditions. The bonds that were once broken have been fully restored, and my family life often feels like a true miracle in an existence that was once so desolate and isolated.

"

# THE REAL GLORY IS BEING KNOCKED TO YOUR KNEES AND THEN COMING BACK. THAT'S REAL GLORY. THAT'S THE ESSENCE OF IT.

VINCE LOMBARDI

# CHAPTER 14

# REDEMPTION

On December 9, 2016, six years after my very first day sober, I walked out of one of Minnesota's state universities as a graduate. I had never thought I'd make it back to college at all, but after five and a half years, I'd graduated with a bachelor's degree in business management and with the highest of honors. I still had no idea what I wanted to do with my career over the long term, but thankfully I had advanced very quickly in my work at a beautiful treatment program in Owatonna. I'd started in 2015 as a treatment technician, an entry-level support position that allowed me to work directly with those early in recovery every day, and before long I had been promoted into a finance role. At that point in life, after three consecutive years of significant loss, I was more intentional about family than I was about my professional plans, and I was okay with that. I had confidence that a career would materialize and I would reach my goal of operating my own business someday, but who knew when the next funeral would come.

The following June, I attended a three-day seminar. My goal in attending was to learn how to better interact with people, not to take things so personally, and to feel more intrinsic value in the things I did. On the surface, life was great. I had made a strong recovery, graduated from school, built new relationships with amazing people in recovery, and more. But deep down, I was still suffering from grief over my broken relationships, distorted thinking, and a bit of anger.

I stood at the front of the room, shaking and scared to be so vulnerable, and shared my intent for the upcoming weekend. "I'm sick of feeling like a jerk, getting upset with people, and being robbed of happiness so many days." It was a relief to share in front of so many people, and it lifted a weight and set me on a path to real progress that weekend.

The change in my mindset started as soon as I heard others begin to share. In front of a crowd of a hundred, one woman broke down as she told the story of being raped and how it had impacted her sense of worthiness. Through her tears, she told us she had never felt like she was good enough after the incident. Another attendee, an older man from Chicago, shared about how he'd lost his sense of worthiness after he received a D on a third-grade math test. Many more stories followed, and I began to see how similar feelings had stemmed from a broad range of events. Whether the root cause was rape, a bad score on a test, or being talked down to by their parents, the result was the same in every person who shared—a feeling of not being good enough, and endless efforts to prove that feeling wrong. Through social media, through career success, through every imaginable channel, everyone was trying to show themselves on the surface as "good enough" to the rest of the world. And in doing so, they were all failing miserably at actually being happy under the surface. I thought I was the only person who had such silly thoughts and feelings of unworthiness, just as years earlier I'd thought I was the only one suffering from the crazy thinking of addiction. Realizing that we were all here trying to do the same thing and hide the same hurts brought me a sense of connectedness and relief I hadn't been able to find in years of effort.

The next morning, driving back to day two of the seminar, I noticed the walls and trees along the interstate. The trees were bright green, reflecting the sun like I'd never seen before. The tall, wooden walls that protected some of the houses from the busy noise of the interstate appeared to me for what felt like the first time. I had driven past them hundreds of times but realized I had never really noticed them. The world slowed down as I watched other cars passing in both directions, and the beauty of nature—the trees, the bright blue sky, the green grass, and even the brown soil—filled my vision. I was experiencing a presence I wasn't accustomed to, and it brought tears to my eyes. The weekend was bringing a new perspective and way of being to my life. At the seminar, I learned how frequently we humans, the most powerful and innovative species on the planet, continue to poison our present, and even our futures, with our pasts. I learned more about presence in those three days than I had in all my prior years of life. I accepted fully that nothing I suffered from today was a result of the things that happened in my past, but rather my inability to see that I was in control of my present state of being. I felt a freedom as strong as the one I'd felt when first relieved of the obsession to drink and use drugs. That freedom opened the door to mending relationships that had long since needed it. This time, I didn't care who was at fault. I wanted to fight for the greater good of family and was willing to do whatever that took.

After my grandpa's funeral, I had managed to reconnect with many of the cousins from his side of the family and build new relationships that we had been missing out on for many years. Eventually, a few of us decided to plan a weeklong trip to northern Minnesota around Labor Day, to re-create the kind of big family reunions my grandpa used to put together when we were kids. The first place we looked at was a perfect fit, so I booked the resort on the spot and a date was set. For the first time in a long time, a large group of our family, about fifty, would be getting together for something other than a funeral or wedding.

At that first family reunion, about thirty of us sat around the fire in Nisswa, Minnesota, on a warm summer night. The fire was crackling, the stars were bright and plentiful, and the air was light and peaceful. Four of our crew started harmonizing, two playing guitar and two singing. The group took turns requesting songs, and the musicians took turns honoring those requests. I stood behind the inner circle of chairs and stared out into the night sky, watching the stars twinkle, and hearing the beautiful ring of the voices and guitar strings. I captured several moments of presence, where it felt like the world stopped for a minute. I thought back to the work I had done in that seminar the year before, especially around my relationships with family, and I was overwhelmed by a sense of gratitude. I looked back to the people circled around the fire, watching everyone joyfully sing along with smiling faces, knowing I had had the privilege of contributing to the occasion, and shed a few tears. I stood in awe at the possibilities that had come from simply taking ownership of my life, getting as authentic as I could, and taking some initiative to build connections again. I realized that without having done that work, I'd simply have gone on showing up at a surface level while being filled with resentment and cynicism on the inside. Family had taken on a new meaning several times in the seven years of sobriety I had gained. But this time was different, and the connections I was building were so much bigger than me and my own interests.

...

I had a strong intuition that my life was meant for something bigger than I could imagine. I knew my greatest value lay in service to others, and that the blessings in my life were directly correlated to the amount of service I committed to doing. I had spent a lot of time over the past few years volunteering in recovery programs, and the work I'd done there, while sometimes tedious and strenuous, had also given me a bigger-picture view of how I might contribute to the world and help a population that needed it more than most. There are so many ignorant views about addiction out there that often the only ones who can unconditionally lend a hand are those who have lived inside those rooms of recovery. I also knew I needed the sense of purpose that came from giving back to keep me in remission from the deadly disease of addiction that had plagued me for so long. Recovery was embedded in everything I did, and I don't know if I'd have made it through my first several years of sobriety without it.

So when my buddy Dan called during my family reunion and said he had a big idea to share, I was more than ready to listen. Over the phone one afternoon, he laid his idea out: He wanted to purchase a house and turn it into a sober home, a place where those in early recovery could live while they tried to get back on their feet. It was a dream scenario to me. I had a lot of ideas about recovery, including ideas around fitness, spirituality, and more, that were difficult to implement in the settings that already existed for those in recovery. Dan and I agreed to meet the next week, along with a couple guys who had pledged to provide the space and real estate, and four others who were willing to put in the work to start a business and operate the home. We knew right away that we were on to something. One meeting led to another, and before we knew it, within just a few months of grueling hard work, we had opened our doors to the first residents. Healing Homes Network was born in 2019, creating a safe space for women to heal and build recovery. The trials and tribulations that came with supporting those in early recovery were plentiful. We saw women relapse regularly, but we also saw them prosper gracefully. Two short years later, in the middle of a global pandemic, my business partner Allison, the only one of the original crew left by that time, and I opened the doors to a second sober home for women.

Healing Homes Network had been a crazy idea—sober housing isn't a moneymaker, it isn't passive, and it isn't for the timid. But we had a vision and a heart for recovery, and that made it more manageable. Creating space for even one woman to have a shot at life made it worth it. That's what I had been given—a shot at life—because of a similar housing option space. It was so meaningful to be giving that back. And before I had even realized it had happened, for the first time in my life, I was a business owner. It was yet another dream come true, but even more importantly, it could and would help fulfill the dreams of others.

...

By 2019, in addition to working with Healing Homes, I had taken on a director-level role with an addiction treatment company that offered comprehensive services for those in recovery. Along the continuum of client needs, the company met necessities such as food and shelter, then treated the core issues around addiction and mental health, and, finally, supported continuing education and employment. The last of those offerings is what made the company especially attractive to me. Housing people and treating their core disorders was, of course, necessary, but I knew firsthand that creating space for purpose and long-term success through jobs and education was what ensured the greatest chance at recovery. When people find purpose, there is a lot less room to revert to old behaviors.

For the first time in my career, in this new role my work was more focused on administrative operations than on client-facing services, but it was still framed by my core value of serving humanity. Rather than supporting recovery by working directly with clients, I supported it by supporting those who did work with clients. Occasionally, though, I'd still get an opportunity to work with clients directly, and one of those occasions reminded me just how badly our world needs grace and humanity.

It was a cold January morning in 2020, and I was at work early as usual. It was about 6:15 a.m., so there were just a handful of staff in the office. As I walked through a conference room toward the stairs to the kitchen to make my typical breakfast—a toasted peanut butter and banana sandwich—a man came running through the front doors screaming, "He's dead, he's dead!"

I dropped my breakfast ingredients on the conference room table and glanced out the front door, where a line of people stood waiting for chemical health assessments. A young woman at the front of the line was kneeling over a lifeless body. I called back to one of my colleagues to find some Narcan, a lifesaving opioid overdose-reversing medication that wasn't yet standard practice to store onsite; and as he ran the other way, I pushed my way through the front door.

"Michael!" the woman screamed, "Michael, no!" With tears falling from her eyes, she shook the man repeatedly, pleading with him to take a breath. I dropped to one knee next to her and asked her what had happened.

"He overdosed!" she cried.

I grabbed the back of the man's neck, lifted his head slightly, and began applying a sternal rub, using the knuckles of my pointer and middle fingers to dig firmly into his chest bone. His neck was warm and sweaty, but his body was lifeless, and his face was a pale gray color. He wasn't responding, and the Narcan was nowhere to be found. The world seemed to stop. What was probably just a couple minutes felt like an hour as I continued to apply more pressure to his chest. Finally, when I least expected it, he let out a little grunt, enough to prove he was still alive. I talked louder and begged him to hang in there, continuing to apply pressure to his chest with my knuckles. And then I heard the most hopeful of sounds—the loud ringing of an ambulance siren. About fifty feet down the road, an ambulance arrived, and a few paramedics jumped out onto the sidewalk.

"We have an overdose—we need Narcan now," I yelled. To my surprise, they didn't move with a ton of urgency, and I never saw them administer the lifesaving medication. The paramedics grabbed the man's body and flopped him around like he was a rag doll, showing very little compassion or care. They took him into the ambulance, where none of us would see him again.

To this day, I have no idea what happened to that man. I was appalled to see how professionals in the business of helping people, especially saving lives, could be so cold and inhumane with someone who clearly needed their empathy. My work in the recovery industry and my personal connection to recovery made it easy for me to see that this man was struggling and needed help. But the incident made it clear that many people simply look at addiction sufferers differently from others. I realized in that moment how critical treatment programs like mine were in the fight against addiction. I knew I was in the right place, fighting alongside some of the best.

...

I spent the next couple years giving my life to that organization, working tirelessly to fix every problem I could. Eventually, I realized my life had become consumed by work, almost as if a new addiction was forming, and I had justified it because I knew how badly people needed help. The company's mission was an honorable one to support, but I knew it was time to rejuvenate my own passion, purpose, and life.

Nearly a decade earlier, I had taken an introduction to business course at Riverland Community College where one of our assignments was to come up with a business plan and present it to our classmates. I came up with a plan to start a speaking business, in which I would manage a stable of speakers who could motivate and inspire crowds by sharing their own challenging personal stories. I knew, from experience, the impact inspirational speaking could have on the speaker and the audience, and I knew there had to be millions of stories out there. I remember thinking how great it would be to bring those stories to others, but I worried that it wasn't an idea others would buy into. I finished the exercise for the sake of the course, then left the idea to die, letting what others might think deter me from pursuing my dream business. Years later, in 2019, I met another man, also named Jason, who made a living speaking, coaching, and training. He had heard me give one of my more powerful speeches at a fundraising event for an organization fighting homelessness in southern Minnesota, and he later convinced me to join the National Speakers Association.

"You're ahead of most people who start in this industry," he said. "You have a natural talent and passion in public speaking, and the story you tell has a way of gripping the audience. Now you just need to build a business foundation so that can become your primary income."

By that point, I had spoken a hundred times or so, mostly at recovery programs, treatment centers, fundraisers, churches, and schools, all without charging a penny. I'd only ever thought about sharing my story with those in or around recovery, and I had been so service-driven that I'd never thought of my life story and teachings being worth money. But I realized that over the years, I'd accumulated a core set of operating principles that not only enabled recovery, but also created happiness and peace in my life, and I knew everyone could benefit from that. The fact that our world needed something different was only becoming increasingly apparent in the early years of the 2020s—with the world plagued by a pandemic, civil unrest, and a growing sense of divisiveness, I knew there was good reason to bring life-changing tools and lessons not just to those in recovery, but to all of humanity.

It had taken almost a decade, but finally my dream, the one I had set aside as silly, grew legs. My personal brand had been building naturally over the years, long before I knew it. Whenever I spoke, I felt a passion, a fire, and an overwhelming sense of filling my bucket that never wavered. Speaking had undoubtedly become my greatest passion—nothing else came close. So I leaned into it, hard and fast. I knew the time was right to create a business that would serve as a space for consulting, training, and speaking. My life was aligned with my purpose, and the possibilities were endless.

"

# WHAT WE CALL THE BEGINNING IS OFTEN THE END. AND TO MAKE AN END IS TO MAKE A BEGINNING. THE END IS WHERE WE START FROM.

T. S. ELIOT

# FULL CIRCLE

Sitting on the patio couch of the pool deck at my new apartment building, I stared out to the west into a clear, starlit night. It was a Minnesota September night at its finest—a cool breeze, crisp air, and a lightness about the atmosphere. Flames rushed through the glass and charcoal rocks in a long, gas-powered firepit. I was wearing a warm, hooded sweatshirt, curled up on a woven, cushioned chair with my legs hanging over the armrest, a foot or so from the bending fire. The flames warmed my feet while my eyes wandered up to the center of the sky. At first glance, I saw three distinct stars forming a long triangle. As I drifted into a presence only afforded by that kind of still picture, I began to see, in the stars, a representation of my life. The brightest of the three was directly above me. It was my starting point, nearly thirty-six years before, when I had sat in a car seat on the bed of a pickup truck and felt at peace with the world. The next star was not far below, and in my mind's eye I drew a line to it, a line that represented my first twelve years of struggling to adjust to life and fit in. The third star was down to the left, down a long line representing the next twelve years. They had been twelve years of relief that turned to pain, and of a hellish journey that promised no escape. But what I hadn't known as I'd traversed that line was that there was one more line in the sky—a line that drew a long climb back to the brightest star in the sky. That long line represented my twelve-year journey of recovery and wellness. It was a journey filled with too many beautiful moments to capture on paper. It was an unthinkable return to possibility. The longer I lay there, gazing at the sky, the more apparent the other stars around the triangle became. They represented wonder, possibility, and freedom, all of which were endless. I knew I had only experienced a small fraction of what this precious life has to offer, and I knew I had only given a small fraction of what I could offer. The next star, wherever it was, was waiting. The next journey was starting. And I was ready for it, whatever it might bring.

"

# IN THE END, THE VALUE OF MY LIFE SHOULD ULTIMATELY BE MEASURED BY THE VALUE I'VE ADDED TO THE LIVES OF OTHERS.

JASON LENNOX

# EPILOGUE

Most recovery programs were based on the idea that once you've found your way, you turn back to help those who are still on the path behind you. Unconditional giving and service are integral parts of recovery. Not only because of the capacity to help others, but also because engaging in unconditional service creates a sense of purpose in the giver that can go a long way toward keeping them sober and happy. Through my early years of recovery, I volunteered at a ton of meetings, served on committees and boards, and even started a recovery meeting in a town that desperately needed it.

But I knew there was more I could do beyond recovery, too. I saw what was happening around the world—disease, homelessness, a misinformed society dropping judgments on those in unfortunate circumstances—and I often found myself asking what I could do to make a difference.

In 2015, I found one answer while watching episodes of ESPN's *My Wish*, which gives children with serious, life-threatening diseases the opportunity to meet their favorite athletes and sports teams. The show piqued my interest in working with children who were seriously ill, and some internet searching led me to the For a Day Foundation, a national organization that served children with cancer and other serious illnesses. A few conversations later, I had begun partnering with the foundation to open a Minnesota chapter. Working with children who had terminal illnesses and watching them play and enjoy their last days with enthusiasm and joy gave me an even greater appreciation for my own life and health. Those kids forced me to reconsider what I saw as "challenges" in my life, and they offered me a new perspective.

In the years since, I've learned again and again that giving back is the best way to stay grateful, to stay focused, and to stay sober. Today, I spend my time as an executive in the behavioral healthcare industry, fighting for change at every level, including in client care, operational processes, organizational management, public relations, and governmental policy. I own and operate two recovery homes, which provide a safe space for people in early recovery to heal and grow. I also own and operate a speaking and consulting business, where I use my technical and people skills to help individuals, organizations, and societies grow in humanity and sustainability. Several years ago, I began blogging to share my story, and that blog eventually evolved into the book you're holding now.

Ultimately, my greatest desire is to use my voice to alter the trajectory of humankind. That might sound grand, but I didn't survive the tragedy of addiction only to play small games in life. I'm committed to showing up to play the biggest games, to make a difference for as many people as I can, in as many ways as I can.

There are still so many misconceptions in our world about addiction. I hope my story illustrates for you how dangerous some of those misunderstandings can be. The idea that recovery is as simple as "just say no" can be a deadly one for people who are still locked in the depths of addiction. For those who are struggling, hearing those words significantly reduces the chances they will ever reach out for help, let alone find long-term recovery. There is a stigma that's been passed down over the years around addiction that makes it incredibly challenging for people to share their realities.

For me, one person who was willing to listen without judgment, and to believe that I really could change, was all it took to finally turn the corner. If you are struggling, or have struggled, with substance use, I hope you're able to find such a person in your own life, and find inside yourself the authenticity to share where you are and where you've been. If you can dive deeply to find your values, connect everything you do to them, and stay steady in your pursuit of a new way of life, salvation is not far away.

If you're watching a loved one struggle, the best way to help them is to find your own values, show compassion, and keep healthy boundaries in place while continuing to support and love them. When a person is struggling with substances, addiction sickens everyone in their circle. But recovery can create health, wellness, and joy for everyone in the circle. Keep your circles intact, stay close, stay strong, and stay hopeful. I hope you leave this book armed with a clear understanding of how complicated the cycles of addiction can be. Through knowledge, compassion, and love, we can all find a better way forward.

My experience through my first dozen years of recovery has come together to form one simple yet powerful personal mission:

to inspire people throughout the world to build and maintain authentic lives that foster peace in the face of chaos, love in the face of hatred, and generosity in the face of self-seeking. When it's all said and done, I believe my life's value will be measured by the impact I've had on those I've encountered. We all leave a legacy that will impact generations to come. Now that you've traversed my journey with me, maybe even connecting it to your own, I leave you with two simple questions to consider as you navigate your life and seek your purpose in our world: If not you, then who? If not now, then when?

# RESOURCES

If you or someone you love is struggling, don't be afraid to reach out for help. The organizations listed below are all wonderful places to start.

You can also reach out to me through my website at jasonlennox.com, or by email at: jason@jasonlennox.com.

**Recovery Self-Help and Support Groups:**

Alcoholics Anonymous: www.aa.org

Cocaine Anonymous: https://ca.org

Crystal Meth Anonymous: www.crystalmeth.org

Heroin Anonymous: https://heroinanonymous.org

Marijuana Anonymous: https://marijuana-anonymous.org

Narcotics Anonymous: www.na.org

Celebrate Recovery: www.celebraterecovery.com

SMART Recovery: www.smartrecovery.org

**Substance Use Disorder Resources:**

Substance Abuse and Mental Health Services Administration (SAMHSA)

—Hotline: (800) 662-4357

—Home: www.samhsa.gov

—Find Treatment: https://findtreatment.samhsa.gov/

Addiction Guide Resources:

    www.addictionguide.com/about-us/resources

Hazelden Betty Ford Foundation:

    www.hazeldenbettyford.org/addiction/what-is-addiction

**Mental Health Resources:**

Emergency: Dial 911

Mental health hotline: Dial 988

National Alliance on Mental Illness (NAMI):

    www.nami.org/Home

American Psychological Association (APA) hotlines:

    www.apa.org/topics/crisis-hotlines

Mental Health America (MHA): www.mhanational.org

National Institute of Mental Health (NIMH):

    www.nimh.nih.gov

**For Family and Friends:**

Adult Children of Alcoholics & Dysfunctional Families:

    https://adultchildren.org

Al-Anon/Alateen: https://al-anon.org

Nar-Anon: www.nar-anon.org/naranon

Partnership to End Addiction: https://drugfree.org

National Institute on Drug Abuse (NIDA) parents and

    educators resources: https://nida.nih.gov/research-topics/

    parents-educators

Hazelden Betty Ford Foundation family and friends resources:

    www.hazeldenbettyford.org/treatment/family-children/

    childrens-program/resources

# ACKNOWLEDGMENTS

I want to acknowledge the amazing team that helped transform a bunch of blog posts into a powerful memoir. First, a special thanks to Christine McKnight, my developmental editor, who had the courage to tell me the truth about my first manuscript—that it needed a complete overhaul—and who had the dedication to see it through a second time. Second, thanks to LeAnna Weller Smith and the team at Weller Smith Design, who turned impossible timelines into reality, and who captured the essence of my story and dreams so magically in the design and layout of this book. Without either of these two, I'm certain I'd still be spinning in circles wondering where to go next.

Many people supported me through the early, middle, and late stages of writing. I'll forever be indebted to my cousin Sarah for inspiring me to start and guiding me through the beginning of the process, and to my life coach Larry for continuing to hold me accountable and pushing me toward realizing the value of this project. And to Kendra, thank you for so graciously extending incredible patience, support, and forgiveness as I trudged through the later stages of this book.

From my earliest days in recovery, I owe significant thanks to Deb and Steve, or Ma and Pa, as I call them, who took me into their home, their family, and their hearts as I found my way through the most challenging times of healing. I also want to thank Rich and Jay, two early recovery sponsors who saw me through the proven steps of recovery that changed my life. Without them, I don't think I'd be alive.

I want to acknowledge my family, especially my mom, Tammi, for sticking through the worst of times and never giving up on me. I'm also grateful for my siblings—John, Dale Jr., and Jamie—for riding out the storm that was our childhood with me, and for the never-ending support as I worked through addiction and recovery. I want to acknowledge my stepfather, Dale Sr., who helped raise me and showed me what change could look like.

For my other dearest family members, I'm so grateful. I want to acknowledge my son Aiden, who's given me a reason to be the father I was never capable of being, and his family for stepping in where I couldn't. I'm forever grateful for my cousins Ben and Audra, who showed up later in my life and continued to encourage me to use my powerful voice to reach as many as possible. For my aunties Dana, Mayra, and Donna, I am so thankful. They helped me get to know my father, who I didn't really get to know while he was alive, through many years of stories and shared love.

My cousin Scott, who lost his life tragically in 2014, had such a profound impact on my childhood years and did everything he could to support me during my worst years. I'll be forever grateful for the memories of our time together.

My grandparents Jim and Donna, who are no longer with us, were the guides I needed all throughout life, and they continue to guide me as I live on without them. I also want to acknowledge others who are no longer with us, especially anyone who's fallen to the deadly disease of addiction. You are a primary reason I keep fighting internally and externally.

I would be remiss if I didn't express my deepest gratitude to all those who've shared their own wonderful words with me as I've written, spoken, and shared my story in many ways. If you've ever left me a comment, a kind word, or shared with me personally, you've made a difference, that I promise.

And finally, I want to acknowledge my father, John Jr. He left us in 2004, at the young age of thirty-nine, after his own decades-long battle with addiction. His life, though relatively short and separate from mine, has given me the fire inside to show the world what possibilities exist when the power of addiction is channeled into a better outlet. My father lost his mom as a teenager, something that crushed him and altered the direction of his life. While it's sad to think about what could have been, I know he's inside every ounce of my being. For you, Dad, I will always fight the good fight.

# ABOUT THE AUTHOR

**JASON LENNOX,** an addiction survivor who found his own recovery after a drug overdose in 2010, is a behavioral healthcare executive, founder and owner of two small businesses supporting organizations and individuals in recovery, and professional speaker and author who has used his story to influence hundreds of thousands of people in his twelve years of recovery. A strong member of the recovery community, Jason has advocated for change in the addiction treatment industry at the levels of individuals, organizations, societies, and government. He's dedicated his life to helping our world better understand how to use authentic ways of being to transform the worst of situations into the greatest of assets.

To learn more about Jason, especially in how he can support you and your endeavors, visit www.jasonlennox.com, where you can find more of his work, hire him for your next event, and follow him on social media.

CPSIA information can be obtained
at www.ICGtesting.com
Printed in the USA
BVHW042130120423
662271BV00006B/57